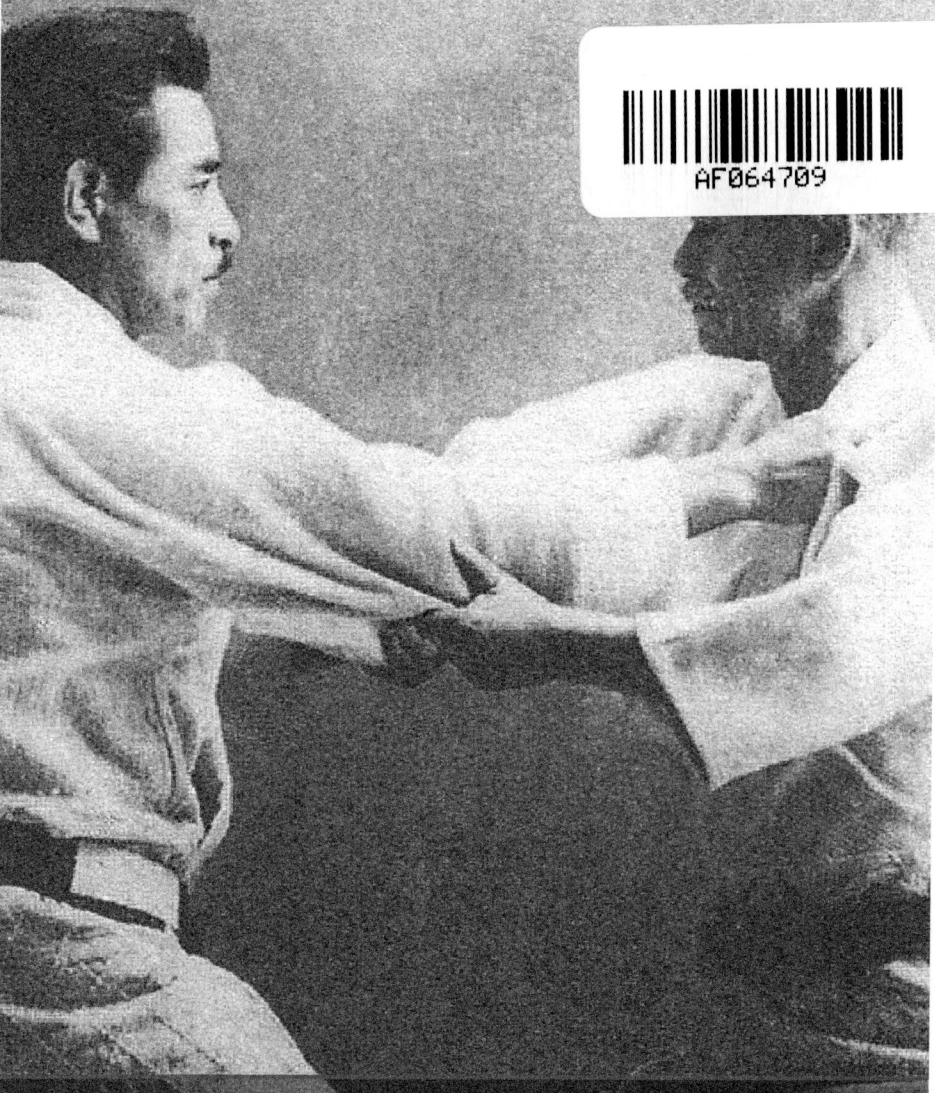

JUDO KATA

• practice • competition • purpose

An Anthology of Articles from the *Journal of Asian Martial Arts*
Compiled by Michael A. DeMarco, M.A.

Disclaimer
Please note that the authors and publisher of this book are not responsible in any manner whatsoever for any injury that may result from practicing the techniques and/or following the instructions given within. Since the physical activities described herein may be too strenuous in nature for some readers to engage in safely, it is essential that a physician be consulted prior to training.

All Rights Reserved
No part of this publication, including illustrations, may be reproduced or utilized in any form or by any means, electronic or mechanical, including photocopying, recording, or by any information storage and retrieval system (beyond that copying permitted by sections 107 and 108 of the US Copyright Law and except by reviewers for the public press), without written permission from Via Media Publishing Company.

Warning: Any unauthorized act in relation to a copyright work may result in both a civil claim for damages and criminal prosecution.

Copyright © 2016
by Via Media Publishing Company
941 Calle Mejia #822, Santa Fe, NM 87501 USA

All articles in this anthology were originally
published in the *Journal of Asian Martial Arts*.
Listed according to the table of contents for this anthology:

Smith R.W. (1996), Vol. 5 No. 3, pp. 60-65
Jones, L. (2005), Vol. 14, No. 3, pp. 72-85
Ebell, S.B. (2008), Vol. 17, No. 1, pp. 28-37
Gatling, L. (2008), Vol. 17 No. 1, pp. 68-77
Jones, L., & Hanon, M. (2010), Vol. 19 No. 4, pp. 8-37
Yiannakis, L. (2011), Vol. 20 No. 3, pp. 92-107
Yiannakis, L. (2014), Vol. 23, pp. 1-13
Jones, J., Savage, M. & Gatling, L. (2014), Vol. 25, pp. 1-45
Jones, L. (2016), In Asian Martial Arts:
Constructive Thoughts & Practical Applications, pp. 86-89

Book and cover design by
Via Media Publishing Company

Edited by
Michael A. DeMarco, M.A.

Cover illustration
Jigoro Kano (right) with his gifted protégé Kyuzo Mifune.

ISBN: 9781893765351

w w w . v i a m e d i a p u b l i s h i n g . c o m

contents

iv **Preface**
by Michael DeMarco, M.A.

CHAPTERS

1 **The Masters Contest of 1926: An Epiphany in Judo History**
by Robert W. Smith, M.A.

7 **Competition, Kata, and the Art of Judo**
by Llyr C. Jones, Ph.D.

22 **Competition Versus Tradition in Kodokan Judo**
by S. Biron Ebell, M.A.

35 **The First Kodokan Judo International Competition and Its Katas**
by W. Lance Gatling, M.A., M.P.S.

43 **The Way of Kata in Kodokan Judo**
by Llyr C. Jones, Ph.D., and Michael J. Hanon, Ph.D.

70 **A Taxonomy of Principles Used in Judo Throwing Techniques**
by Linda Yiannakis, M.S.

85 **Rhythm, Patterns, and Timing in Martial Arts as Exemplified Through Judo**
by Linda Yiannakis, M.S.

100 **Kodokan Judo's Self-Defense System: Kodokan Goshin-jutsu**
by Llyr C. Jones, Ph.D, Martin P. Savage, B.Ed., and W. Lance Gatling, M.A., M.P.S.

164 **The Logic of Kodokan Judo Kata**
by Llyr C. Jones, Ph.D.

168 **Index**

preface

The practice of judo katas has changed over time as a result of perceived purpose. The chapters in this anthology were written by seven authorities in judo history and practice. Their writings clarify the purpose of kata and thus its mode of practice and their place in competition.

In 1926, a contest occurred in which thirty-seven of the finest judoka in Japan competed before the Emperor Hirohito. The first chapter by Robert W. Smith details the techniques utilized by each master and also compares their skills with today's judo practitioners.

The next two chapters by Dr. Llyr Jones and Biron Ebell deal with the transmutation of judo over the decades. Both authors give ample support that the original guidelines have evolved into competitive sport resulting in a substantial decline in the number of adults practicing judo.

Where does kata stand in judo practice today? Dr. Lance Gatling reports on The First Kodokan Judo International Competition (2007). He outlines the background of the competition, the competitors, the motivations for this competition, the historical development of judo katas, and their importance to the correct study of judo.

Dr. Llyr Jones' next chapter has two objectives: to explain the purpose of kata in judo, and to critically evaluate the concept of kata championships. To achieve these objectives, Jones offers personal comments, observations from rare Japanese source material, as well as insight into the thinking of world-renowned judo experts.

Linda Yiannakis provides two insightful chapters. Her first chapter presents a conceptual framework for examining principles of judo throwing techniques. The principles are classified as primarily structural, operational, or contextual in nature. In her second chapter, she points out that martial artists are acutely aware of the need to develop a sense of timing for the best possible moment to apply techniques in free play or contest. This chapter examines some critical features of patterns and rhythms in a variety of contexts and provides a few basic exercises for the development of awareness and use of rhythm, patterns, and timing in judo.

Jones, Savage, and Gatling present an in-depth study into Kodokan Goshin-jutsu—a Kodokan judo exercise formally established in 1956 to teach the principles and techniques of self-defense against unarmed and armed attacks, and to meet modern lifestyle needs. Their chapter reviews the place of Goshin-jutsu among the Kodokan katas, and then summarizes the history its creation. A description of the exercise's structure and technical contents follows, along with an in-depth explanation of its principles and associated teaching and learning challenges. This also includes a review of the most reliable learning texts in Japanese, English and selected other Western languages.

Kodokan Goshin-jutsu's performance aspects are considered next. An objective assessment of its practical self-defense effectiveness follows, before finally conclusions are drawn.

The short final chapter by Dr. Jones is on Kodokan judo's Nage-no-kata (forms of throwing) and Katame-no-kata (forms of control). Their study helps facilitate the development of free practice (randori) skills.

Many look at judo studies as including three dimensions: free-practice, competition, and forms. Kata practice is vital to the other two. If you are involved with judo, this anthology will deepen your purpose and inspiring your practice.

Michael A. DeMarco, Publisher
Santa Fe, New Mexico
September 2016

Notes

chapter 1

The Masters Contest of 1926
An Epiphany in Judo History

by Robert W. Smith, M.A.*

Mifune Kyuzo executing a "corner drop" (*sumiotoshi*).
All photos courtesy of R. Smith.

*Note: This chapter was first written in 1953. Readers must take this into consideration to clearly understand the chronology of events and the respective ages of the practitioners discussed.

    The Biblical phrase "There were giants in those days" is exemplified by the judo masters of the Kodokan. Some of their past exploits indicate an extraordinary mental and physical capacity.
    In 1926, a contest (*shiai*) occurred that was the equal of any preceding and without peer in any following tournament. Thirty-seven of the finest judoka in Japan competed before the Emperor Hirohito. But the championship eliminations were eclipsed by the appearance on the mat of eight of the greatest judo masters in history:[1] Mifune Kyuzo, Tabata Shotaro, Goto Ichizo, Kurihara

Left to right: Mifune Kyuzo, Tabata Shotaro, Kurihara Tamio.

Tamio, Samura Kaichiro, Iizuka Kunizaburo, Isogai Hajime, and Nagaoka Shuichi.[2] All were highly-graded teachers well along in years, probably not at their contest best, but willing to demonstrate their ability in the face of age and its concomitant slowing reflexes. The four matches in which they participated are an epiphany in judo history.

Mifune vs. Tabata

Mifune (5 foot 3 inches, 135 pounds) was dwarfed by the stocky Tabata (5 foot 6 inches, 190 pounds). Mifune was a decided underdog—to everyone but Mifune, that is. No sooner had the two taken hold than Mifune, with no show of strength, lashed out with a foot sweep (*okuriashi-hari*), causing Tabata to stumble and temporarily lose his balance. Tabata recovered before Mifune could follow up his advantage. Both held lightly, stood straight, and moved gracefully. Tabata took the offensive with a well-placed blocking foot-lift pull throw (*sasae-tsurikomi-ashi*), which caused Mifune's body to rock precariously. Quickly regaining his balance, Mifune shortly after attempted a circle throw (*tomoe-nage*), but this was blocked easily by Tabata. With three minutes remaining, Tabata tried a side sacrifice throw (*yoko-sutemi*), failed, and immediately tried it again. Mifune's feet left the mat and *ippon* (full point) seemed a certainty. Midway in its arc, however, Mifune's body turned like a cat and he rolled onto his side. It was a close escape, and Yamashita Yoshitsugu, that whitehaired exemplar of pure judo, the referee, called out nothing. Shortly afterward, time ran out and Yamashita declared the match a draw.

Goto vs. Kurihara

Next, Goto and Kurihara, each 39 years of age, squared off. Immediately Kurihara, renowned in the Kyoto area for his groundwork, tried a circle throw

Left to right: Iizuka Kunizaburo, Samura Kaichiro, Isogai Hajime.

(*tomoe-nage*) and, when this failed, attempted a body drop (*taiotoshi*). Goto shook off both attempts easily. It was obvious to the spectators that Kurihara was trying to lead Goto into *ne-waza* (groundwork).[3] But this time, Goto, seeing his antagonist supine, leaped into groundwork. Kurihara turned from underneath at Goto's approach and began a strangle. Adroitly, Goto escaped and stood up. On again taking hold, Goto speedily struck with a lift-pull hip throw (*tsuri-komigoshi*). But Kurihara remained upright. After several feints, Kurihara tried a combination of smaller inner reap (*ko-uchi-gari*) and side sacrifice (*yoko-sutemi*) throws, against which Goto defended successfully. With time expiring, Kurihara essayed a volley of throws–circle, big outer reap, and side sacrifice–but in his concern over the time, his coordination was lacking and Goto never lost his balance. After time expired, referee Yamashita called the match a draw.

Samura vs. Iizuka

On this day in 1926, two men, still alive (both have since died) and graded tenth-dan, the highest of the high, met in the third match of this epic series. Samura, pupil of the inimitable Yokoyama Sakujiro—perhaps the greatest judoka of all time–was pitted against Iizuka who, at 60, was the oldest active master at that time. Both Samura and Iizuka were cautious and neither attempted anything in the first three minutes. The crowd was hushed and silent. Iizuka shifted from a basic natural to a left natural posture. Samura feinted as if to pull Iizuka into groundwork and then sat down into a circle throw. Iizuka tumbled atop him as a result of this. They stood up. Samura tried a circle throw again, this time with more precision and better placement, and Iizuka fell. But it was neither quick nor crisp, and Yamashita, the referee, said nothing. As time expired, Iizuka was trying to bring Samura into groundwork, but Samura resisted successfully. Yamashita called the match a draw.

Yamashita Yoshitsugu, referee of the 1928 Masters Contest. He taught President Theodore Roosevelt at the White House (1903-1907). Right: Kano Jigiro, founder of judo.

Isogai vs. Nagaoka

The last bout of the day brought together the two greatest experts of that era, Isogai and Nagaoka. The spectators leaned forward on the edge of their seats. Here was the zenith of judo!

With a fierce *kiai* (spirit shout), Isogai seized Nagaoka's jacket. There was no aimless walking about, both moved with the utmost caution. Isogai stepped in beautifully with a side sacrifice throw (*yoko-sutemi*), but, just as beautifully, Nagaoka evaded the attempt. In escaping, he did not push, but rather skipped outside the trajectory of Isogai's pull. Isogai stood up and they again took hold. While neither tried a great deal, it was clear that the minds of both were racing apace. Suddenly, Nagaoka spun into a leg wheel (*ashi guruma*) but Isogai did not waver. A silence permeated the crowd. Time was on the move and the watchers knew that neither of the masters could be content with a draw. They were right. After some maneuvering, Nagaoka tried his terrible favorite left-side sacrifice throw (*hidari-yoko-sutemi*). This was the technique that had enabled him to reach the judo heights. It was yoko-sutemi that succeeded when other throws (*te*) failed. But it did not succeed this day against Isogai. That master did not lose his balance. Isogai's backers breathed easier. At this point, referee Yamashita declared the match over and announced it a draw. Probably neither Nagaoka nor Isogai was content but each had to be in the face of the merit of the other.

The principals of these bouts lived to further the concepts developed by Kano Jigiro, the creator of judo. Mifune, our "grand old man," is on the wrong side of seventy, but still engages in daily free practice (*randori*) and teaching. Before his death, Tabata wrote an occasional article for the Kodokan monthly magazine *Judo*. Kurihara (ninth-dan) lives in Kyoto and in 1951 traveled to Europe with Kano Risei's Kodokan party, where he gave masterly kata demonstrations with his prize student Awazu Shozo (sixth-dan). Awazu, predictably, is also a ground specialist and currently assists Kawaishi Mikonosuke (seventh-dan), the leader of French judo since 1936.

Samura, at an advanced age, teaches tactical theory through a regular section in the Kodokan Judo journal. In this, his esteemed collaborator was, until his recent death, the incomparable Nagaoka. So far as this writer knows, Iizuka is still living, and a member of the faculty of a Tokyo university where he has taught judo for many years.

Nagaoka has passed on. Shortly before his demise, a picture of this mighty master, walking in a flower garden with a cane much in evidence, appeared in a French publication. I experienced a mild pang on seeing it, for not too long before this I had seen Nagaoka in the 1950 Kodokan judo film, in which he tossed a younger, heavier opponent with ease and grand *waza* (techniques). *Tempus fugit*, and "before one realizes it, one is in the sere and yellow leaf," as E. J. Harrison, quoting the Bard, commented in a recent missive. And it is a pity.

Isogai is gone also. But he left a legacy in the form of two judo texts. I have been unable to ascertain the present status of Goto (eighth-dan).

So much for the men. Now, what of their techniques? I think the reader will readily discern at least two points emerging from the above descriptions of their bouts:

1) The predominant use of tomoe-nage and yoko-sutemi, throws now seldom achieved or even tried.
2) The few throwing techniques tried during the course of a match.

In respect to the first point, the implications are easy to grasp. All of these masters had the "feel" of sacrifice and foot techniques to such an extent that a throw such as tomoe-nage or yoko-sutemi was as much a major weapon for them as the inner thigh throw (*uchi-mata*) is for Yoshimatsu Yoshihiko[4] or the big outer reap (*osoto-gari*) is for Daigo Toshiro[5] at the present. In other words, they relied more on subtle unbalancing than on strength.

Regarding the second point, the masters "thought" during a match. Only when there was a concrete likelihood of a full point was a throwing attempt made. The fact that no *kaeshi-waza* (counterattacking techniques) occurred and the ease with which they escaped their antagonists' overtures attest to good initial unbalancing and body control (*tai-sabaki*) beyond the ken of most judoka.

In closing, I venture the opinion that these eight masters came to the art with no extraordinary physical equipment. Nor did they reach their high estate in the judo hierarchy by remarkable brainwork. Without a doubt, they all held in common (though in varying degrees, certainly all high) a will to win. This will sufficed to make their ordinary bodies perfect servants of their nimble minds, minds which had been made sharp by repetitious physical practice.

We see a complementary, reciprocating process at work—the will driving the mind, which works the body, which in turn, refurbishes the mind and, in the end, rewards the will. The process is exemplified in each of the masters we have discussed, and if the reader must have a moral, it is probably this: the merit of the masters began—and continues to begin—with the will, and in the end, their merit was and is proportionate to that will.

Acknowledgement

Special thanks to Warren Conner, Russ Mason, and Joseph Svinth for reading and commenting on this article in its preliminary stages.

Notes

[1] The summaries of these bouts were taken from *Showa Tenran Shiai* (Judo and Kendo Matches Before the Emperor in the Showa Period), Tokyo: Kodansha, 2 volumes, 1934, 1981 pages. The writer thanks Ben Ishii (first dan, Seattle) for the translation. The article itself was first written in 1953 and appeared in the *Budokwai Judo* quarterly (London).

[2] The personal names cited are rendered in the conventional Japanese style, with the surnames first.

[3] Ground techniques allowed in judo include holding techniques (*osae-waza*), joint-locking techniques (*kansetsu-waza*), and choking techniques (*shime-waza*).

[4] Yoshimatsu won the All Japan Championships in 1952 and 1953.

[5] In 1950, Daigo was the youngest man ever to be awarded a sixth-dan. He was 24 at the time. He was noted for various reaping throws and won the All Japan Championship in 1951.

chapter 2

Competition, Kata, and the Art of Judo

by Llyr C. Jones, Ph.D.

Illustration by Oscar Ratti.
© 2001 *Futuro Designs & Publications*.

Introduction

The word "judo" comes from a combination of two Japanese words—*ju* meaning gentle or supple and *do* meaning path or way. This literally defines judo as the "gentle way."

At the level of first principles, the essence of Kodokan judo is turning an opponent's strength against himself and overcoming the opponent through skill rather than sheer strength (Kano, 1986). This theory is captured by the Japanese expression *ju yoku go o seisu*—usually translated as "softness overcomes hardness," "flexibility overcomes stiffness," "gentleness controls strength," or "win by yielding."

Watching the seemingly effortless combination of grace, technique, and power of a true judo expert in action, it would be very easy (but very wrong) to underestimate the intense physical and mental demands that judo makes upon its exponents. Achieving excellence in judo demands considerable single mindedness. Achieving mastery of all of the throwing, grappling, and striking techniques that makes up the system demands intensive and demanding training over an extended period of time under the guidance of an experienced and knowledgeable teacher.

Judo has been well established in the West since the early 1900's and is now practiced in almost every country in the world. The aim of this paper, however, is to question the direction that judo has taken in the West (especially in the United Kingdom) and to challenge whether a significant re-orientation is now required. Where specific statistics or statements are used to support an argument, data and examples from the British Judo Association (BJA)—the national governing body for the Olympic sport of judo in the United Kingdom—are used.

The State of Judo Today

As a starting point, it is worthwhile stating the definition of judo as provided by the *Kodokan New Japanese-English Dictionary of Judo* (Kawamura and Daigo, 2000):

> **Judo:** A martial art formulated by Jigoro Kano based on his reformulation and adaptation of several classical jujutsu systems as well as his own philosophical ideals.

Such a definition may not resonate well with the image of judo promoted by the official accredited national governing bodies—i.e., those belonging to the International Judo Federation (IJF)—the majority of whom seem to be actively encouraging the distancing of judo from its martial arts origins. In these early years of the 21st century, it is difficult to challenge the view that in the West (and in the United Kingdom in particular) judo is promoted one dimensionally, as a combat sport—organized around championships and competition—often for competition's sake. To reinforce this sporting dimension, the competitive style of judo is often referred to as *Olympic Judo* or *Performance Judo* (a style in its own right).

A direct consequence of the leadership and policies of the accredited judo governing bodies is that, for the majority of judo practitioners, judo is now just about medals and prizes. These bodies measure the health of their country's judo simply in terms of results at major championships and accordingly focus their investment only on the handful of elite athletes who have the potential to be World or Olympic medalists. Bethers (n.d.) recognizes this issue:

> It seems that some modern judo leaders have narrowed the objective of judo to only "Contest Proficiency." For many, world-wide judo has become equated with contest proficiency. Although this belief is today wide-spread, it is the very thing that Dr. Kano warned against throughout his life. Dr. Kano stated, "Judo should only be a means to the end of skill

and principles for higher self-development, and any 'drift' toward 'contest' judo as the 'sole' interpretation of judo should be carefully regulated." This "drift" has become a major focus among many well intended judoka [practitioners], but in the minds of many sensei [teachers], technique has suffered and judo has become (more often than not) a sport in which "win at all costs" is the underlying objective.

It is evident that the strategy of focusing on Performance Judo must now be challenged, as judo today is an activity in decline. In the United Kingdom, this is manifested by decreasing adult membership of the British Judo Association—75% of the BJA membership is under the age of 16 (British Judo Association, n.d.)—and the continuing lack of consistent and substantial success of British judo players in international competition despite all the effort directed to this end.

It is a matter of additional concern that the governing bodies have overwhelmingly biased their rank promotion structures (i.e. grading) toward accelerating the grade advancement of those who are successful in competition, with often only lip service being plaid to the breadth and depth of an individual's technical judo knowledge. Again, Bethers (n.d.) writes:

> This emphasis on "Contest Proficiency" has caused the true meaning or purpose of judo to be unclear and somewhat out of proportion to what was intended by Dr. Kano. This problem is surfaced nowhere more clearly than in "notion" that contest victories are rewarded with rapid rank promotions.

Currently there is little prospect for grade advancement for those who (through age, physical condition, or personal preference) wish to practice judo as an art as opposed to a sport. This is, of course, with the notable exception of the promotions that governing body officials and administrators seem to receive as a matter of course. The risk one runs with such a policy is a resultant judo hierarchy that is both one-dimensional in its knowledge and skewed in its priorities.

It is especially disappointing that those judo players who prefer to focus their study on the more traditional and technical aspects of judo (e.g. forms or *kata*) have become tagged with the label recreational players—implying that they are somehow inferior to contest players and not worthy of attention or recognition.

Back to Basics

This author and other writers (Watanabe, 2003; Burkland, 1998) advocate the thesis that judo in the West has lost its way and that there is a real need for it to return to its martial art roots. In doing so, the author's aim for this paper is not to decry the considerable merits of Performance Judo—indeed success in contest over several traditional jujutsu schools was key in establishing Kodokan judo as an effective combat system (Kano, 1986). Rather, it is to argue that judo based solely on sport is not judo *in toto* and that the original and arguably truer meaning of the art lies elsewhere.

Elementary research will reveal that the underlying concept of judo as envisioned by Kano was that it was to be a means of (cooperative) physical and social education—in simple terms, a training for life. Kano captured this principle of mutual welfare and prosperity via the maxim: you and I shining together (*jita kyo ei*, mutual welfare and prosperity) (Kano, 1986).

Indeed, with the overwhelming majority of those now practicing Performance Judo, it is reasonable to conclude that mainstream contemporary judo has now deviated significantly (and quite possibly permanently) from Kano's original ideas. Smith (1999: 221) notes:

> The popularization and spread of judo has weakened Kano's base so greatly, I see no chance of it ever recovering. Judo is now merely a jacketed wrestling sport. The competitive has ousted the cooperative.

Bates (n.d.) argues that judo has two essential components—martial and art. The martial component of judo can be related to combat through the way of the warrior (*budo*)—the contemporary representation of which is competition (*shiai*). In preparation for contest, the modern judo player focuses on the development of physical conditioning and fitness, motivation, tactics, and technique for the sole purpose of securing victory. Conversely, art can be defined as technical excellence and understanding of techniques developed through repeated practice (*uchi-komi* and *nage-komi*), free-practice (*randori*), and kata.

Judo is, of course, both martial and art, but today the concept most people have of judo is martial. Martial represents but one small element of judo, yet almost without exception, most judo teachers focus on developing their students' contest prowess and many believe it unnecessary to practice or even know any kata.

Rediscovering Kata

In the most general sense, any cooperative judo training between partners—e.g. a sequence of combinations or counters etc.—can be considered kata. However, a greater degree of focus is provided in a dictionary of judo (Kawamura and Daigo, 2000), which defines kata as follows:

Kata: Formal movement pattern exercises containing idealised model movements illustrating specific combative principles.

Kata is not unique to judo—it is recognized as a valuable training drill in most Japanese martial arts. The exact nature of kata training, however, varies from art to art. For example, karate kata is a solo form (like shadow boxing), whereas the judo kata are usually performed with partner—each partner having a specific role and performance objective depending on the kata. In judo, there are kata for throwing techniques, groundwork techniques, self-defense, as well as others that illustrate the fundamental principles of judo (Kano, 1986; Otaki and Draeger, 1983; Leggett and Kano, 1982; Kawaishihi, 1982; Fromm and Soames, 1982; Ohlenkamp, 2005).

For completeness, a comprehensive list of the kata practiced in judo follows, together with a summary description of each (Ohlenkamp, 2005). Illustrations of techniques from the seven most common kata are provided in Figures 1 to 7.

Figure 1 (top): Nage no Kata. **Figure 2** (bottom): Katame no Kata
© Photography by Bob Willingham. bob@twoj.org

Note that not all of these kata were created by Kano or at the Kodokan and, as such, some are not official Kodokan kata. Note also that the last six kata in the list are seldom practiced outside Japan and, even in Japan, few judo players would be familiar with them.

- **Nage-no-kata:** The kata of throws. Includes examples of hand, hip, leg, and sacrifice throws (Figure 1).
- **Katame-no-kata:** The kata of grappling. Includes examples of holds, strangles, and chokes and joint locks (Figure 2).
- **Kime-no-kata:** The kata of decision. This is the traditional judo self-defense kata. It includes both standing and kneeling defense against empty handed, knife, and sword attacks using strikes, chokes, joint locks, and throws (Figure 3). Kime-no-kata is also known as Shinken Shobu no Kata (combat forms).
- **Kodokan Goshin-jutsu:** The modern Kodokan self-defense kata (Figure 4). It includes defense against empty hand, knife, stick (jo), and pistol attacks using strikes, joint locks, and throws.
- **Ju-no-kata:** The kata of gentleness. It includes a number of attacks and defenses demonstrating the efficient redirection of force and movement (Figure 5).
- **Itsutsu-no-kata:** The kata of five principles. This kata is intended for the demonstration and practice of body movement (*tai-sabaki*) and for the application and redirection of energy as in nature (Figure 6).
- **Koshiki-no-kata:** The ancient kata. This kata has its origins in Kito-ryu Jujutsu and demonstrates the techniques of fighting while wearing armor (*kumiuchi*), and is intended to illustrate the ancient origins of judo techniques (Figure 7).
- **Go no Sen-no-kata:** The kata of counters. This kata includes counter throws for a number of common techniques.
- **Kaeshi no Kata:** An alternative kata of counters.
- **Seiryoku Zenyo Kokumin Taiiku:** The national exercise based on the principles of maximum efficiency. This kata is atypical of judo in being a completely solo kata and comprises a variety of striking and kicking techniques.
- **Kodokan Joshi Goshin-Ho:** The Kodokan's women's self-defense kata. This kata includes a number of escapes from holds and grabs, some basic striking techniques, and one throw.
- **Renkoho:** The kata of arresting techniques. This kata includes a number of control and submission holds useful in restraining criminals.
- **Kimi Shiki:** The kata of decision. This kata emphasizes the use of body movement in responding to attacks and includes both kneeling and standing defenses against empty hand, knife, and sword attacks.
- **Shobu-no-kata:** The kata of attack or contest.
- **Go-no-kata:** The kata of the proper use of force. This kata is the complement to the Ju no Kata and dates back to the earliest days of the Kodokan where it was used as a training drill.

Figure 3 (l.): Kime-no-kata. **Figure 4** (center): Kodokan Goshin-jutsu. **Figure 5** (r.): Ju-no-kata.

Figure 6 (l.): Itsutsu-no-kata. **Figure 7** (r.) Koshiki-no-kata.

In nearly all martial art styles, forms are used as training tools from the novice stage upwards. In judo, however, its significance has long been under-emphasized and kata practice is now largely confined to very high grades or those who are not contest-inclined. It is a tragedy of modern judo that, in the headlong rush into Olympic-type competition, most ranked black belt holders regard forms as an anachronism of little relevance to competition that should be discarded. The late Charles Palmer (then BJA president) anticipated this situation when he wrote his 1982 foreword to Leggett and Kano's kata text (Leggett and Kano, 1982):

> ... too much emphasis is being placed on winning at all costs. Not enough time is being spent by judo players on acquiring the vital self-discipline necessary to proper performance of the sport, and the ability to continue enjoying it later in life after the ability to win contests has decreased.

It was particularly insightful of Palmer to recognize that Performance Judo is age limited. Such sport judo is the domain of the young, whereas Kodokan judo (especially kata) can be done up until a very advanced age.

A direct consequence of kata not being part of the normal activity of most judo clubs is that the availability of people with the required knowledge and teaching skills is very limited. Today some of the better known judo forms are in serious danger of becoming extinct.

For the reader's interest, teaching sequences for two techniques from *Kodokan Goshin-jutsu*—two-hands hold (*ryote dori*) and uppercut (*ago tsuki*)—are provided in Figures 8 and 9. Similarly, teaching sequences for two techniques from the *Koshiki no Kata*—strength dodging (*ryokuhi*) and water wheel (*mizu guruma*)—are provided in Figures 10 and 11. These sequences were performed under the technical direction of world masters international kata judge Bob Thomas.

Two-Hand Hold

8a Bob Thomas (right) and Eddie Cassidy approach each other. **8b** The attacker steps with his left foot forward into the proper distance to simultaneously grab the defender's wrists and tries to strike with his right knee to the groin. **8c** The defender bends his right arm hard toward his chest to free it and, **8d** continues his motion to strike the attacker's right temple with the knife-edge of his right hand. **8e** The defender grabs the attacker's right wrist from the top with his right hand and applies an armlock (*kote hineri*). He steps back with his right foot and opens his body to his right. The defender clamps the attacker's right arm under his left arm and twists the attacker's wrist. The attacker is forced to submit, or have his arm broken.

Uppercut

9a Eddie Cassidy (right) and Bob Thomas approach each other. **9b** The attacker steps with his right foot forward into the proper distance to simultaneously throw a right uppercut. The defender steps slightly back with his left foot and deflects the attacker's uppercut from below with his right hand. **9c** Immediately, the defender grabs the attacker's right wrist with his right hand, thumb down, and the attacker's elbow with his left hand. He twists the attacker's wrist away from him and pushed the attacker's elbow toward his face. **9d** While keeping his arm extended and locking the attacker's elbow, the defender takes a big step forward with his left foot and throws the attacker forward.

Strength Dodging

10a Eddie Cassidy (right) and Bob Thomas approach each other. **10b** The attacker steps forward, left foot then right, and attempts to grab the defender's belt with a cross grip—right hand uppermost. The defender simultaneously pulls the attacker's right arm forward. **10c** The defender pulls the attacker forward to his right side, while placing himself behind the attacker. He holds the attacker's elbow bringing the arm upwards while holding the attacker's upper left arm. **10d** The defender pulls the attacker backward to the right side while dropping to his left knee as the attacker falls to the ground. **10e** As the defender kneels, the attacker sits up, keeping his legs spread with straight legs, toes up.

Water Wheel

11a Eddie Cassidy (right) and Bob Thomas approach each other. **11b** The attacker steps forward with his left foot then right, and attempts to seize the defender's belt with a cross grip—right hand uppermost. The defender simultaneously pulls the attacker's right arm forward. **11c** The attacker resists by pulling backward. The defender responds by changing his direction of movement, lifting the attacker's right arm, and presses it toward the attacker's forehead.

11d The defender moves in closer and unbalances the attacker by bending the attacker at the waist with his left hand and pressing the attacker's right arm against his own forehead with his right hand. This makes it easy to push to attacker backward. **11e** The defender bends the attacker backward and the attacker responds by resisting and straightening up and inclining forward a little. The defender then takes advantage of the attacker's forward inclination and changes his grip. He also adjusts the position of his feet. **11f** The defender then falls backward and executes a sacrifice throw. **11g** The attacker rolls over the defender in mid-air. **11h** The attacker comes onto his feet and the defender remains on his back with legs and hands spread for about three seconds. This concludes the action.

The Importance of Kata

To gain a true understanding of judo as envisioned by Kano, it is necessary to look beyond competition to kata. This author believes that the link between judo's past and future is embodied in the accurate teaching of kata for it is only in kata that the totality of judo has been preserved—especially the traditional and more dangerous self-defense techniques that are also present in judo.

Kano identified two types of training for judo—forms and free-practice—and held the firm belief that these two training systems had to co-exist in parallel. Kano envisaged kata being the laboratory for judo development and free-practice as the testing ground (Otaki and Draeger, 1983).

In particular, Kano developed kata to demonstrate the principles of judo and to provide a type of training in which students could examine techniques under ideal circumstances—thus penetrating their very essence.

Through repeated practice, the techniques of the various forms can be performed without thinking and, in the extreme, kata can unify mind, body and spirit—arguably the purest goal of a martial art. Indeed, many judo practitioners claim to have experienced moments of enlightenment and insight as a result of a perfect kata performance. Notwithstanding the subjective spiritual dimension, it is certainly true that all judo players involved can derive a great deal of self-satisfaction from a high-quality kata performance and the associated focus, awareness, attention to detail, and self-discipline demanded. Furthermore, students and teachers should also not overlook the significance of forms as purely a part of general instruction: kata teaches movement, timing, and coordination. Kata was, and remains, the basis of judo, and provides the vehicle for perfecting many throws, holds, and other techniques in a finer way than individual technical instruction or general free-practice.

Critics of kata argue that forms bear very little resemblance to competition in that the techniques are performed at a standard pace with a predetermined outcome in an overly symbolized style. It is not widely known that most high-grade Japanese teachers still emphasize the importance of kata for a judo practitioner's development and that many consider the study of the *Randori no Kata* (*Nage no Kata* and *Katame no Kata*) in particular to be an essential part of training for the highest level of contest success (Watanabe, 2003; Otaki and Draeger, 1983; Kawaishihi, 1982).

In their seminal text *Judo Formal Techniques*, Otaki and Draeger (1983) state:

> Sufficient kata study and practice impose a well-defined technical discipline on the judoist, one that is unattainable by only randori and contest methods. This discipline, instead of hampering the judoist,

actually frees him from undue restrictions, liberates his bodily expression in movement, and teaches him economy of mental and physical energy. This process can only be understood through experience, and only through kata performance can judoist come to appreciate judo in its fullest sense.

Kawaishi (1982) reinforces the point:

> The kata will temper the combative ardor of the young performer and will undoubtedly also enable him to discover the reason for certain errors he commits in competition... Thus the kata is a valuable source of technical progress.

Accordingly, the contest player should consider kata as part of his training for physical, mental, and contest proficiency in an identical fashion to free-practice and conditioning work, etc.

Concluding Remarks

Given the substantial decline in the number of adults practicing judo, it can be argued that there is a real need to re-examine the value system associated with judo. A way must be found to retain and ideally attract more adults into judo. As part of this exercise, the emphasis between the martial and art strands of judo should be examined simultaneously because the strands should not be separated. In doing so, one would be well served to note Burkland's (1998) conclusions:

> Judo must focus on its heritage as a traditional martial way by emphasising randori [free-practice] and kata as the primary training vehicles for the development.... Shiai [competition] must be returned to its proper perspective and cannot be allowed to dominate our thinking and our efforts.

Gleeson (1976) showed that there was a close connection between the three dimensions of judo and argued that free-practice, competition, and forms were all essential to each other. Gleeson recognized that, through ignorance and neglect, artificial boundaries had been built between the dimensions, preventing people from moving easily from one to another. Gleeson also acknowledged the need to deconstruct these boundaries for judo to prosper.

A similar idea has been expressed metaphorically by relating judo to a three-legged stool—the three legs being free-practice, competition, and forms (Kin Ryu Judo, n.d.). The metaphor proceeds to argue that if any one leg is removed, the stool falls over. Therefore, without equal emphasis on all three elements, judo will be flawed. The interested reader requiring a further perspective on Kodokan judo—including the introduction of a concept of four overlapping areas for study (i.e. physical education, sport, unarmed combat, and philosophy) is also directed to Anderson (n.d.).

Additionally implicit in the re-evaluation of judo's value structure is a real need to reassess and reformulate the promotion system. In doing so, a fundamental tenet of Kano's philosophy should be at the fore:

> It's not that you are better than someone else that's important,
> but that you are better than you were yesterday.
> – British Judo Association, 2004

The principles expounded in this paper are already starting to come to the fore with the emergence of a number of bodies dedicated to the preservation of the traditional techniques and values of judo as a martial art. Such bodies could provide a more natural home for the judo purist than the official sport-orientated governing bodies.

Judo today faces a crisis no different than that facing Kano Jigoro in 1882 when he founded judo from jujutsu. In evolving judo from jujutsu, Kano endeavored to preserve jujutsu's fundamental elements unless they be lost forever. In the West, similar radical steps are needed to re-establish and preserve the heritage, traditions, and forms of judo that were Kano's true genius.

Bibliography

Anderson, V. (n.d.). The four pillars of judo. *Fightingarts.com*. http://www.fightingarts.com/reading/article.php?id=146

Bates, A. (n.d.). Classical judo—Time to realise. In *Tokushima Budo Council Official Bulletin*, No. 79.

Bethers, B. (n.d.). Training in Kodokan judo—"One perspective." *Martial Arts International Federation (MAIF) Traditional Kodokan Judo Program.* http://www.maintlfed.org/resources/kodokan.html

British Judo Association. (2004). *One of Britain's most senior judoka inspires south coast youngsters.* http://www.britishjudo.org.uk/home/ percysekine.php

British Judo Association. (n.d.). *British judo facts and figures.* http://www.britishjudo.org.uk/media/documents/BritishJudo-Facts_000.pdf

Burkland, R. (1998, Spring). Judo: Martial way or modern sport. *Shudokan*

Martial Arts Association Newsletter. http://www.michionline.org/smaa/articles/burkland_judo.html

Fromm, A. and Soames, N. (1982). *Judo: The gentle way*. London: Routledge and Kegan Paul.

Gleeson, G. (1976). *The complete book of judo*. Toronto: Coles Publishing.

Kano, J. (1986). *Kodokan judo*. Tokyo: Kodansha International.

Kawaisihi, M. (1982). *The complete 7 katas of judo*. Woodstock, New York: The Overlook Press.

Kawamura, T. and Daigo, T. (2000). *Kodokan new Japanese-English dictionary of judo*. Tokyo: Kodokan Institute.

Kin Ryu Judo Club. (n.d.). *The basics of judo*. http://www.kinryu.org.uk/judobasics.htm

Leggett, T. and Kano, J. (1982). *Kata judo*. Slough, Berkshire, UK: W. Foulsham and Co.

Ohlenkamp, N. (2005 February 3). Forms of judo (kata). *Judo Information Site*. http://judoinfo.com/katamenu.htm

Otaki, T. and Draeger, D. (1983). *Judo formal techniques*. Tokyo: Charles E. Tuttle Co.

Smith, R. (1999). *Martial musings: A portrayal of martial arts in the 20th century*. Erie, Pennsylvania: Via Media Publishing.

Watanabe, K. (2003). *World masters judo championship kata booklet*. Richmond Hill, Ontario: World Master Judo Association.

chapter 3

Competition Versus Tradition in Kodokan Judo

by S. Biron Ebell, M.A.

Jigoro Kano (1860-1938), founder of judo.

Introduction

Practitioners of oriental martial arts are sometimes surprised to find that *katas* (formal prearranged form [Otaki and Draeger, 1983: 441]) are actually part of Kodokan Judo. This belief seems to be based on the opinion—probably also shared by the general public—that judo is a sport; plain and simple (Nurse, 2004). A belief further reinforced by the fact that judo is an Olympic sport. Today, however, most people generally do not consider it to be a martial art and, some senior judo practitioners would rather not have the term "martial art" be applied to judo at all (Sadej, 1999: 2-3; Schell, 1999: 2-3); despite judo's obvious historic connection to the Japanese martial traditions. This view, I feel, may be turned on its head when the history and stated purpose of judo is taken into account. In fact, when considered in detail, judo is actually a modern *budo* or martial way (Draeger, 1974), whose purpose far exceeds sport or competition. Therefore, this short chapter will briefly touch on several important topics including:

- The historical foundation of judo
- The learning and practice of judo
- How the current focus on competitive judo is narrowing its purpose and eroding principles and practices espoused by its founder
- How economic priorities are driving judo's evolution away from the interests of its majority participants

Judo History and Purpose

Judo, or Kodokan Judo, as it is more properly known, is a synthesis of several styles of jujutsu by the 19th century Japanese visionary and educator, Jigoro Kano (1860-1938). Kano was born October 28, in Mikage, which is now part of Kobe city. In 1874, he entered the Tokyo School of Foreign Languages, where he mastered English to the point that all of his personal notes and later, his budo journals, were written in that language (Stevens, 1995: 11-12). Ironically, his journals have been published in Japanese, but not English!

In 1877 he became a student at Tokyo University and fell victim to "bullies" and "ruffians." It was about this time that he began his study of Tenshin Shin'yo-ryu jujutsu under the tutelage of Hashinosuke Fukuda (1829-1880). This he did in spite of being admonished by his family and colleagues to forget jujutsu because "...times have changed and such things are no longer useful" (Stevens, 1995: 14-15). By this time in history, jujutsu had fallen into disrepute for a number of reasons, not the least of which was because it had become a means of public spectacle and bravado—losing the honor that it and other martial arts had enjoyed for many centuries in Japan (Kano, 2005: 20-21). However, Tenshin Shin'yo-ryu jujutsu was comparatively new but had a reputation of being an effective means of self-defense (Draeger, 1974: 113). It specialized in *atemi waza* (techniques for striking anatomically weak points of the body) and *katame* or *ne-waza* (grappling techniques).

Within the first year of Kano's training, his teacher died, but he continued his study under the direction of Masamoto Iso (1818-1881), the son of the school's founder. Following Iso's death in 1881, Kano began studying Kito-ryu jujutsu under Tsunetoshi Iikubo (1835-1889). An extremely esoteric and philosophical art, Kito-ryu specialized in *nage-waza* (throwing or projecting techniques) (Kano, 2005: 22-23; Draeger, 1974: 113). In 1883, Iikubo awarded Kano a Kito-ryu teaching license.

In 1882, after five years of diligent study, Jigoro Kano established his own martial art he called "Kodokan Judo," synthesized primarily from Tenshin Shin'yo-ryu jujutsu, Kito-ryu jujutsu, and others. *Kodokan* usually is translated as "school for studying the way" (Kano et. al., 1986: 16). He adopted the term "judo" to differentiate his martial art from jujutsu (Kano, 2005: 18-22). *Ju*, implies flexibility or adaptability, as it did with jujutsu, but the suffix "*do*," suggests a more sophisticated purpose for the art. "Do" is an esoteric term generally implying a way of life, a way of thinking, and/or a way of living (Kano, 2005).

But judo did not, by any means, spring from Kano's head fully formed. It progressed slowly from the original concepts of the *jutsu* forms he studied, and continues to evolve to this day. One of his greatest innovations was devising a curriculum—an organized, graded sequence of study that insured both safety and structure for students (Donohue, 2005: 26) and an efficient means of learning that differed from that used in jujutsu (Kano, 2005: 33-34). As Nurse (2004) points out: "Perhaps his [Kano's] greatest innovation was (sic) the teaching of *ukemi*, or 'break-falling,' before a new student begins the study of technique. This ensures that when a novice is thrown, he or she has already learned how to land safely and efficiently on the mats without danger. This was a significant departure from many of the jujutsu systems Kano had examined previously, where students were thrown—sometimes having their limbs deliberately wrenched in the bargain—and had to land as best they could."

Kano's Raison D'etre for Judo

Kodokan Judo Principles and Aims (Kano et. al., 1986: 20-25), state clearly the primary objectives of judo are physical fitness, studying attack and defense, and moral training. Kano (2005: 23) states: "...I divided it [judo] into three parts: its use as a fighting method (martial art), as a training method (physical education), and as a method of mental training (including the development of the intellect and morals and the application of judo to everyday life...)."

The ultimate aim of physical fitness and physical education, Kano states, is to "...make the body strong, useful and healthy while building character through mental and moral discipline, ...making efficient use of mental and physical energy... (while progressing) ...toward the goal of promoting health, strength and usefulness" (Kano et. al., 1986: 20). He also observed that sports are competitive in nature and as such, overemphasize a less than balanced physical development to accomplish their particular ends, while doing little or nothing for the moral discipline of their participants.

Kano emphasized training the whole body as well as mind and moral fibre, for the good of society. He saw the means to accomplish this while learning the arts of attack and defense. To do so safely, judo players require the cooperation of their training partners. And in order to continue to have training partners, they must consider each other's well being. Doing so instills a sense of responsibility for ones training partners and by extension, ones fellow man. This important concept was distilled in Kano's dictum of "*jita kyoei*" or Mutual Benefit and Well-being, which advocates "...perfecting one's self and benefiting the world (Brousse and Matsumoto 1999: 84; Kano, 2005). So, Kano envisioned the use of judo as a means of achieving a healthy body, a moral sense of mutual respect and responsibility, and the ability to apply self defense techniques should they be required in day-to-day life using modified techniques of attack and defense from jujutsu.

Another, but nonetheless important dictum of Kano was, "*seiryoku zenyo*," which translates to mean "putting your energy to work most efficiently," or "maximum efficiency," directs the physical execution and understanding of judo technique. This dictum advocates "...that no matter what the goal, in

Illustrations by Oscar Ratti.
© *Futuro Designs & Publications.*

order to achieve it, you must put your mental and physical energy to work in the most effective manner" (Kano, 2005: 43). In other words, in all endeavors, whether in judo or daily life, efficiency in action and thought are sought as an ideal.

Judo as Sport

Referring to the modern Japanese sword art of *kendo*, Kiyota (2002: 1) identifies sport as "...a structured human activity carried out in leisure time for the purpose of recreating the human personality." Further, he directs us to a statement by Joseph W. Elder, who says sports include three components: competition (with an opponent), physical activity, and established rules. If these definitions are accepted, then for the most part, much of judo is truly practiced as a sport, but the overarching philosophical and moral priorities advocated by Kano, significantly differentiate it from other sports.

Learning Judo — Randori, Kata and Shiai

Judo is normally practiced in three ways. Foremost, there is *randori*. Originally, both Kito-ryu and Tenshin Shin'yo-ryu jujutsu used *randori*, in which ". . . the two players did not compete with each other, but rather trained together to improve their art. This was permitted only after proficiency was attained in kata" (Kano, et. al., 1986: 141). And, it was in the concept of randori that Kano's genius shown. Most *shin budo* (modern martial ways) even today are practiced primarily as kata. Kano significantly broke with tradition when he made randori a priority in judo study.

Randori is a form of sparing or free exercise, where judo players are at liberty to freely practice their judo skills against a resisting opponent. The objective is to develop both attack and defense tactics, but within judo's rules of engagement. In order for students to be able to freely engage each other, Kano found it necessary to select and modify jujutsu techniques (*waza*) so they could be safely practiced in this manner. So it was in 1895 when the Kodokan established a graded curriculum of throwing techniques (*nage-waza*) known as the *Gokyu no Waza*. This was revised in 1920 and today 67 nage throwing techniques are recognized by the Kodokan (Daigo, 2005: 9).

Ideally there are no winners or losers in randori! This is where spirit and fighting skills are developed and honed. As Kano et. al. (1986: 142) state: "The ultimate goal of randori is to develop the ability to rapidly cope with changing circumstances, to build a strong and supple body, and to prepare mind and body for competition. ...Unfortunately, in many dojo today randori is not practiced as it should be. One reason is the stress on training for competition. ...The resulting contest-style judo is far from ideal."

With randori, judo players practice their techniques without restraint, seeing directly and without doubt, the full effect of their techniques. In fact randori differentiates judo from most other modern martial arts where the full effects of techniques must be restrained for safety reasons.

Second, judo is practiced as *kata*. Most things Japanese are learned as *shikata* or "the way of doing things" (De Mente, 2003: 1). This is a practice "that had been ritualized or sanctified over the centuries" (De Mente, 2004: 73). Traditionally, all day-to-day activities are initially learned in a kata-like manner by rote or repetitive practice. As De Mente (2003: 4) states: "...the Japanese kata-ized their whole existence. Practically nothing was left to chance or personal inclination. The kata factor applied to everything...."

With kata a formal presence in most Japanese behavior, it is not surprising to find katas in their martial arts. In this regard, katas are forms to be followed assuring that a precise body of knowledge is transferred from teacher to student. It is a kind of template to be followed both in learning and performance. Judo is no exception, as katas are an important aspect of learning and practice.

Judo katas are formal, prearranged forms of attack and defense including techniques such as striking techniques that are not allowed in randori. It is in these katas that the martial art aspect of judo is learned and practiced. This aspect of judo is not sport. Further, as judo players are not in competition in kata study, the katas provide the opportunity to continue practicing judo well into old age (Kano, 2005: 141-142). In judo, then, katas function to: direct the correct performance of technique; provide a controlled, predictable environment wherein techniques may be practiced and perfected; allow the study and practice of techniques that have practical self-defense application; maintain physical fitness after competition training is no longer feasible. And by striving for the perfection of technique, discipline and patience are honed.

But in the strictest sense, *uchi-komi* (practice drills) are katas as well (Otaki and Draeger 1983: 40, 428). It is by doing *uchi-komi* that the basic technical details of techniques are learned. Under a teacher's strict supervision, the rote, sometimes monotonous repetition of techniques embed the motor skills that are necessary for judo practitioners to properly execute judo's techniques. Often during a training session, a technique may be repeated hundreds of times. Because judo players cooperate in this form of practice, and actions are pre-arranged, agreed upon and repetitive, this learning process is a form of kata.

To understand judo as a Japanese art requires that its katas be studied. If judo is considered to be a tiny thread in Japan's cultural tapestry, a tapestry learned as *shi-kata*, then to know and understand judo in the Japanese context, one should know and understand its katas. In western *dojos* (training halls), katas are usually perceived as an inconvenient hurdle necessary for promotion. De Mente (2003: 14) points out that there is an interesting dichotomy between Japanese and Western attitude toward katas: "The Japanese were traditionally conditioned to get their pleasure from conforming to kata, from doing things in the prescribed manner. One of the affects of this conditioning was to make the Japanese process-oriented instead of result-oriented."

Western society hurries toward clearly defined end results that symbolically mark the completion of a body of work, such as a university diploma or black belt. But, for most things Japanese, the process of learning takes priority over the final product: in the case of judo, diligent, ongoing study and practice takes priority (at least in theory) over achievement of rank or competitive success. Whether this continues to be so in Japanese society today is a moot point.

Third, there is *shiai*. It is competition that includes referees, adherence to rules, etc. The rules themselves are rather complex. Like most modern combat sports, winning is symbolic. In judo, a contest is decided when a contestant successfully throws an opponent from a standing position mostly on their back with speed, force, and impetus. For this he or she receives an *ippon* or single point that ends the contest. If the contest moves to the ground, an ippon may be scored by controlling the opponent on their back for 25 seconds, or by obtaining a submission using an effectively applied choke or arm-lock, all within a rather concise set of rules.

The ippon is awarded for techniques achieved in contest that would presumably incapacitate or injure an assailant in an uncontrolled combat situation. Like many other martial arts, judo's techniques were considered to be effective in real combat. The ability to produce an ippon or *wazari* (almost ippon) in contest translates to being able to develop an effective attack, or defend one's self, if needed—an important historic component of Kano's concept of judo (Kano, 2005: 23).

Prior to 1972, only ippon and wazari, were awarded. To achieve an ippon in competition required tremendous determination and spirit. It's not easy to throw or immobilize a less than willing opponent. To receive ippon, it was all or nothing. Today, not only have the criteria for ippon been reduced—requiring less force and less speed—but two other scores lower than wazari are now awarded. Of course, competitors have adapted to these new scoring options by designing their techniques to achieve these lower scores and still win their matches, a fact decried by some (Takahashi, 2005: 20). In fact, the new scoring regime has reduced the emphasis on "ippon judo." As Daigo Toshiro (2003: 151), observes, today you can be a winner without ever "taking ippon." Likewise, Kano (2005: 133) observes: "...in competition or in fighting, feeling proud of yourself after winning by inconveniencing your opponent does not fulfill the spirit of judo. ...If you do not win by using waza superior to those of your opponent or by turning his waza against him, this cannot be said to be a true victory."

With the reduced emphasis in contest on "taking ippon" and winning by "inconveniencing your opponent," one can only imagine what might happen if such techniques are attempted in an uncontrolled adversarial situation. Without "speed, force and impetus," a genuinely dangerous situation may ensue. The adversary may merely recover from momentary embarrassment to retaliate to the serious detriment of the judo player. It follows from this that reducing the criteria necessary to win a shiai contest, also reduces the inherent skills of the practicing judo player that may be required in real combat. True enough, Kodokan Judo historically is already four or more times removed from the reality of the battlefield, but to condone a reduction in requirements for winning contests continues to erode its already reduced potency as a means of attack and defense.

Shiai and the Championship

It is in *shiai* that judo players apply all their skills in an effort to defeat an opponent. Shiai is traditionally a tool used to test a judo player's progress and expertise against others of similar skill. As such, shiai provides an opportunity for personal and private assessment of progress: one that is not usually concerned with public acknowledgment. The only person with a vested interest in shiai success, other than the judo player, is his or her instructor. The shiai was, and still is, an occasion for teachers to evaluate students' technique, spirit, and sportsmanship. In fact, a successful shiai sometimes results in a judo player being awarded immediate grade advancement, known as *batsugun*.

But, call the *shiai* a "championship," and competitive rational changes. A "championship" sets the scene for the public acknowledgment of achieved prowess over others. Competition, then, becomes an affirmation of superiority among peers and is no longer only a self-evaluation tool of progress in skill. The change is subtle, but significant, moving from an opportunity for self-evaluation, as found in shiai, to one of self-aggrandizement as an acclaimed, recognized champion (Bowen, 1999: 53). Though the objective of both shiai and championship is to win, the public celebration of winning changes the emphasis from personal, private success, to public acknowledgement, adulation, and fame. And, human vanity being what it is seems to favor fame over self-satisfaction.

Sport Heroes and Social Status

Saul (1992: 506) mentions that seeking "excellence" in sport is an endeavor to move up the class system "with the king of the best on top." It is a seeking of celebrity, and our society seems to "give power to the stars themselves" as a result of public notoriety, no matter however it was received, achieved, or perceived. With respect to sports excellence, Saul (ibid.) observes "we have taken to celebrating competition as a self-evident value." What Saul seems to be saying is that sporting excellence is an excepted way of achieving perceived celebrity so as to move upward in a fictitious social system. The reality is that with almost all amateur sports—judo included—there is little or no financial or social benefit derived from competitive success. This is particularly true of Kodokan Judo where few (if any) professional opportunities exist post-heroism, and where public memory of competitive success, if understood at all, is transitory in the extreme. Occupying the pedestal of heroism merely creates the inherent challenge of those who follow to knock the hero from his/her prominent place; something that is bound to happen given time, age, and the challenge of youth.

Competitive priority has driven judo to evolve inexorably. The administrative focus of the International Judo Federation (IJF), the governing body of world judo, has, and continues to sharpen in the area of competition. One need only glance at their web site to infer that competition, competitive results, and elite competitors are their priority.

This priority is further reflected by contest rules that have increased in complexity over time and the continuing need to more clearly articulate how contests are conducted. Compare, for example, the rather brief 1953 Kodokan rules preserved by Koizumi (1960: 157-165), and Kobayashi and Sharp (1956: 99-102); the 1961 rules (Ishikawa and Draeger, 1962: 291-298); the 1967 Contest Rules (IJF 1967: 20-22); and the 63 page, 14500 word, "Refereeing Rules" of 2003, as they are now called (IJF, 2003). One of the reasons contest rules have become increasingly more complex is because of the need to assure "equality of chances" in competition (Brousse and Matsumoto, 1999: 42).

Take for example the relatively simple description of judo uniform found in earlier rules which describes the general size and make-up of the jacket, pants, and belt (Koizumi, 1960: 157-165). Contrast this with current regulations where detail includes such minutiae as to how it should fit, amount of overlap of the lapel, length of sleeve relative to contestants arm length, etc. Such detail reflects the inherent struggle among judo players to obtain a small competitive advantage over their opponents, and the rules that attempt to assure the contestants' "equality of chance."

Judo and the Olympics

Judo and the International Olympic Committee (IOC) have enjoyed a long association. As Nurse (2004) states: "...in London in 1933, Dr. Kano spoke of his desire for a world judo federation and the dissemination of Kodokan Judo teachings throughout the world as a means of aiding in achievement of world peace. Already he had become Japan's first representative on the International Olympic Committee (1909), as well as the first president of the newly formed Japanese Amateur Sports Association (1911)." One may easily understand why Kano wanted judo to become part of the Olympic movement considering their similar objectives. The Olympic Charter established by Pierre de Coubertin states:

> ...the goal of the Olympic Movement is to contribute to building a peaceful and better world by educating youth through sport practiced without discrimination of any kind and in the Olympic spirit, which requires mutual understanding with a spirit of friendship, solidarity and fair play. ...Olympism is a philosophy of life, exalting and combining in a balanced whole the qualities of body, will and mind. Blending sport with culture and education, Olympism seeks to create a way of life based on the joy found in effort, the educational value of good example and respect for universal fundamental ethical principles.

Both of these statements essentially duplicate the high moral intent of Kodokan Judo and the wishes expressed by Kano that judo function to promote world peace and benefit the world (Brousse and Matsumoto, 1999: 84; Kano, 2005).

Kano's dream that judo become part of the Olympic Games was realized in 1964 when the Olympics were held in Tokyo. Thus began a relationship that has been a mixed blessing to Kodokan Judo. As Holme (1995: 38) points out: "Just after the Munich Olympics there were major changes in the rules. The powers that be had realized that, to attract sponsors, television viewers had to be appeased."

Regarding the role of advertising revenue, the IOC (2005) itself observes: "Television is the engine that has driven the growth of the Olympic Movement. Increases in broadcast revenue over the past two decades have provided the Olympic Movement and sport with an unprecedented financial base. ...TV rights fees continue to account for approximately 50 percent of Olympic revenue."

Regarding participant Olympic sports, the IOC (2005) states: "While conserving their independence and autonomy in the administration of their sports, International Sports Federations seeking IOC recognition must ensure that their statutes, practice and activities conform with the Olympic Charter."

The International Sports Federation concerned with judo is the IJF. From the above, rather contradictory statement by the IOC, the IJF is expected to meet certain criterion in order to comply with Olympic needs. Further one of the IJF's aims is "To support and maintain the ideals and objectives of the Olympic Movement" (IJF, Mission Statement: Aims 2006).

From the above statements, it follows that one of these criteria is to assure television viewer interest and sponsor endorsement. Many of the rule changes mentioned before are the result of the need to make judo more viewer-friendly and increase "spectator appeal" (Takahashi et. al., 2005: 7, 15, 17). The IJF has gone to great lengths to accommodate this (Takahashi et. al., 2005: 7). For instance, traditionally, contestants wore a white or red sash over their belts to aid referees in tracking who scored what. Now, contestants wear either white or blue judo uniforms. This innovation was introduced by the IJF to make it easier to differentiate the contestants on TV, much to the chagrin of traditional Japanese judo practitioners (Takahashi, 2005: 15). On the positive side, the contrasting colors also make refereeing easier. Though not thought to have serious consequence to contest, contestants wearing the blue judo uniform seem to be statistically winners more often than those wearing the traditional white one (IJF, 2006/05/04). The reason for this is still being debated.

Though the IJF, not the IOC, determines the rules of the game, it seems that the rules change all too frequently. This makes it difficult not only for the competitors themselves to know what are appropriate tactics and techniques, but even referees find it difficult to keep abreast of changes (Holme, 1995: 37-45).

The emphasis currently placed on competitive excellence and result has caused judo to divide into two different camps—"recreational" judo and "Olympic-style or Performance" judo. This conceptual and practical dichotomy is having great impact on judo practice (Jones, 2005). This is perhaps a natural consequence of the need to win in the Olympic arena, causing a change in training priority, method and focus. As a result, athletes train extremely hard in a limited number of judo and related techniques that provide the best opportunity to win, while eschewing most of judo's 67 or so techniques. Though this extreme training results in a low general knowledge of judo, frequent injury, early retirement, etc., contemporary judo has, indeed, switched its emphasis from the learning process to achieving an end (De Mente, 2003:

14). This is causing a not too subtle schism between competitors and recreational judo players that is reflected in the priorities of judo's governing bodies.

As Jones (2005: 75) points out, recreational judo is demeaned as somewhat inferior and, "...judo players who prefer to focus their study on the more traditional and technical aspects of judo (e.g. forms or *kata*) have become tagged with the label recreational players—implying that they are somehow inferior to contest players and not worthy of attention or recognition."

However, the vast majority of practicing judo players are involved in recreational activity. In terms of philosophy, recreational judo would seem best equated with the tradition of ongoing learning, physical fitness, and the moral ideals espoused by Kano (2005).

The final position of *kirioroshi* (downward cut), one of the kata (form) found in Kodokan Judo's *Kime-no-kata* (forms of decision). Also known as *Shinken Shobu no Kata* (combat forms), this kata incorporates attack and defence techniques, such as striking techniques and counters to weapon attacks, as shown here. Competitive Olympic judo does not permit the use of striking or weapons. The complete Kodokan curriculum may only be experienced if kata are included as part of regular judo practice. Biron Ebell and Milton Jones (*uke*) demonstrating. *Photography by Brook Jones.*

The competitive priority of "Olympic Judo," leaves the unfortunate impression in the public eye that in order to participate in judo, one must engage in elite competition. It is viewed as another competitive sport and that seems to be where it is ultimately headed. However, the competitive imperative deflects focus from judo's primary objectives established by Kano in the late 19th and early 20th centuries. Yes, by normal process, it has evolved to be somewhat different than it was over a century ago. But as mentioned before, judo is a component of world culture. Unlike organic species that are born into the world with only their genes to prepare them for the vagaries that the environment presents and their ultimate evolution or extinction, judo's "genes" are its participants. These "genes" have the benefit of a collective memory and purpose and, unlike organic species, its evolution can be directed by knowledge of the past and a perception of what judo should be in the future. So instead of bowing to the needs of a disinterested minority TV public and in turn, the profits of advertisers, judo must remain the property all judo practitioners—competitors, recreational judo players, and their teachers. All should play a role in determining how judo should evolve.

With changes in rules to accommodate spectator understanding and IOC sponsors, the nationally driven need to win, and the loss of historic purpose, judo is in danger of coming full-circle and becoming what jujutsu was in the 19th century. Without intervention by judo's governing bodies and instructors, it stands the chance of assuming the same low status that Kano found jujutsu in 19th century Japan (Kano, 2005: 136). In fact, the use of the term "martial art" in the "ground and pound" cage wrestling of so called "mixed martial arts (MMA)" demeans the higher purpose, not only of judo, but of other budo usually included in the martial art genre. Keep in mind that the term, *martial art*, has been misappropriated and is not legitimately affiliated with the kind of demeaning public display found in the MMA cage sports.

On the contrary, Kodokan Judo should cling tenaciously to any, or all of the terms: martial art, martial way, or budo in reference to itself. All these terms reflect a glorious tradition and greater goals than found solely in sport. As Jhoon Rhee (1998), the father of American Taekwondo, states unequivocally, "I call martial arts without philosophy, street fighting...." Oriental martial arts are generally grounded in moral and ethical codes that abhor violence, shun public titillation and display, and are somewhat offended or entertained by the self-aggrandizement of so called masters or cage-match winners. As Donohue (1998: 27) observes "...the real purpose of the martial arts is to forge spirit." And so it was, is, and should continue to be for Kodokan Judo!

Acknowledgment

The author extends special thanks to Milton Jones (3rd-dan) and Henry Epp (6th-dan) who read and commented on earlier drafts of this manuscript.

References

Brousse, M. and Matsumoto, D. (1999). *Judo: A sport and a way of life*. Seoul: International Judo Federation.

Daigo, T. (2005). *Kodokan Judo throwing techniques*. Tokyo: Kodansha International.

DeMente, B. (2003). *Kata: The key to understanding and dealing with the*

Japanese! Boston: Tuttle.

DeMente, B. (2004). *The Japanese samurai code: Classic strategies for success.* Boston: Tuttle.

Donohue, J. (1998). *Herding the ox: The martial arts as moral metaphor.* Wethersfield, CT: Turtle Press.

Donohue, J. (2005). Modern educational theories and traditional Japanese martial arts training methods. *Journal of Asian Martial Arts,* 14(2): 8-29.

Draeger, D. (1974). *Modern bujutsu and budo. The martial arts and ways of Japan: Volume 3.* New York: Weatherhill.

Holme, P. (1996). *Get to grips with judo.* Dorset, England: Blandford.

International Judo Federation (2006, April 21). International Judo Federation Mission Statement http://www.ijf.org/rule/rule_role_mission.php#4

International Judo Federation (2006, May 4). The color of judogis: Wear blue if you have the choice. http://www.ijf.org/board/board_view.php?Page=1&SearchSelc=&SearchText=&Idx=293

International Olympic Committee (2005, Dec., 28). The International Olympic Charter. http://www.olympic.org/uk/organisation/missions/charter_uk.asp

Jones, L. (2005). Competition, kata and the art of judo. *Journal of Asian Martial Arts,* 8(3): 72-85.

Kano, J. (2005). *Mind over muscle: Writings from the founder of judo.* Tokyo: Kodansha.

Kano, J., et. al. (1986). *Kodokan Judo.* Tokyo: Kodansha.

Kiyota, M. (2002). *The Shambhala guide to kendo.* Boston: Shambhala.

Nurse, P. (2004, November 12). The beginnings of Kodokan Judo, 1882-1938. http:\\www.fightingarts.com/reading/article.php?id=53

Otaki, T. and Draeger, D. (1994). *Judo formal techniques: A complete guide to Kodokan Randori no Kata.* Boston: Tuttle.

Rhee, J. (1998). *The mystic origins of the martial arts.* A&E Home Video. A&E Television Networks.

Sadej, A. (1999). Should we promote judo as a martial art? Commentary in: *Yudansha Journal: Official Publication of Judo Canada,* 5(1): 2-3.

Saul, J. (1992). *Voltaire's bastards: The dictatorship of reason in the west.* New York: Penguin Books.

Schell, C. (1999). Commentary in: *Yudansha Journal: Official Publication of Judo Canada,* 5(2):2-3.

Sidney, J. (Ed.) (2003). *The warrior's path: Wisdom from contemporary martial arts masters.* Boston: Shambhala.

Stevens, J. (1995). *Three budo masters.* Tokyo: Kodansha.

Takahashi, M. and Family. (2005). *Mastering judo.* Champaign, IL: Human Kinetics.

chapter 4

The First Kodokan Judo Kata International Competition & Its Katas

by Lance Gatling, M.A., M.P.S.

First Kodokan Judo Kata International Tournament program showing Jigoro Kano, the founder of Kodokan judo, demonstrating Ju no Kata.
All photographs © 2007 Lance Gatling.

The first world judo kata competition was held on Saturday and Sunday, October 27 and 28, 2007 in Tokyo, Japan, at the Kodokan, the headquarters of worldwide judo. There, 78 judo players from seventeen different countries, representing hundreds of years of judo experience, participated. Thirty-nine teams competed in four different forms (*katas*, or prearranged formal exercises) performed before five-member panels of twenty expert judges from thirteen different countries. Those teams were either seeded by regional international judo associations or were winners from regional competitions over the past year in the Pan-Am, European, African, and Asian Judo Unions. Eight teams from Japan, two competing in each kata, were chosen from top performers in the All-Japan Judo Federation's All-Japan Judo Kata Competition earlier in 2007. Like some judo competitions, there was no age or weight discrimination. Unlike other judo competitions, judo kata competitions were not segregated by sex.

But what role do the katas play in judo, and why are they important today?

Judo is comprised of relatively modern adaptations of selected techniques from numerous traditional styles of Japanese jujutsu combined with newer techniques. Since establishing the Kodokan in 1882, Professor Jigoro Kano, the founder of judo, and his technical instructors modified traditional jujutsu techniques into a sporting, competitive, rule-defined, modern martial way (*budo*). While originally constructed to help teach a total way of life, judo continued to evolve. Today, in most countries, competition plays the largest role in judo, much larger than originally envisioned, and partially as a result, today's judo is different from the original judo of 120 years ago.

Therefore, arguably the purest form of the early judo and its jujutsu origins are preserved not in the competition, but rather in its oldest katas. Perhaps the purest presentation of these forms worldwide is during the annual Kodokan kata national contest in Japan, so everyone knew the competition was tough for international competitors.

In his opening speech, Yukimitsu Kano, president of both the Kodokan and the All-Japan Judo Federation, and grandson of Jigoro Kano, noted that the founder stressed that judo must be studied through both free sparring (*randori*) and kata, comparing them to the grammar and composition of judo. He congratulated the contestants on their interest, skills, and long hours of practice. He also noted growing interest in judo katas worldwide.

Opening address by
Kodokan President Yukimitsu Kano.

Modern judo primarily trains via basic technique (*kihon*) practice and free sparring, as well as periodic competitions (*shiai*). Unfortunately, in the view of judo purists and traditionalists, most dojo typically seldom practice katas. While modern judo techniques are safe enough to practice via free sparring or competition; traditionally, jujutsu's more dangerous techniques were and are still practiced in pre-arranged katas, not via randori or shiai. This is because the traditional no-holds-barred jujutsu techniques still practiced in the judo katas are incapacitating if not lethal—including knife-edged hand slashes ("chops"); chokes; joint breaks; head-first body slams; eye gouges; stomps; kicks; and club, knife, and sword attacks. This may be judo's greatest innovation: the modification of these dangerous jujutsu techniques to enable safe, competitive free practice of a deadly art; in fact, taught and performed correctly, judo is statistically one of the world's safest contact sports.

For this competition, four of the main Kodokan katas were chosen; *Nage no Kata* (throwing form), *Katame no Kata* (grappling form), *Kime-no-kata* (decision form), and *Ju no Kata* (flexible form).

Nage no Kata is typically shown in every kata competition because it demonstrates the core of modern judo, with samples of all the main throwing techniques. Every Japanese judo practitioner from 1st-degree (*dan*) black belt is required to demonstrate increasing proficiency and depth in this kata, which was compiled around 1884. Kano was an advanced practitioner of both Tenshin Shinyo-ryu and Kito-ryu jujutsu, which provided many techniques to the Kodokan judo repertoire.

The original *Nage no Kata* was later modified and expanded, largely by adding more rapid, agile moves afforded by the wear of modern, lightweight judo clothing (*judogi*) rather than the traditional, top-heavy cumbersome moves of armored warriors. The attacker of the technique (*uke*, "giver") strikes, grasps, and shoves, ever modifying the attacks to adjust to the previous defense. The defender (*tori*, "taker," "receiver") responds with hand, hip, foot, sacrifice, and side sacrifice throws. They repeat all fifteen techniques from both left and right sides for a total of thirty throws (and thirty jarring falls for *uke*).

The Japanese teams in the *Nage no Kata* were the winners in the annual Kodokan Kata Taikai national competition earlier in 2007. Japanese teams from across the country, winners of a series of regional competitions, performed four different katas.

Kime-no-kata (decision form) is a combative kata from 1888. Appropriately for the early Meiji era (1868-1912) when it was established, it starts with eight armed and unarmed attacks from the formal, seated position (*seiza*), and ends with twelve standing attacks using holds, fists, a wooden knife, and a wooden sword (*bokken*). Judo's jujutsu roots are evident in this kata, in which *tori* uses strikes, joint locks, strangles, and throws to defeat the attacker.

Robert Ivers and Robert Maurency (Australia)
showing Kime-no-kata defense against a knife attack.

Nage no Kata teams from Japan, Spain, and Italy.

Katame no Kata (grappling form) was compiled between 1884 to 1887, and was largely influenced by Tenshin Shin-yo-ryu jujutsu. It can be difficult for the layman to follow because the action is all floor grappling: *tori* demonstrates pins, joint locks, and chokes to immobilize the supine *uke*, who then attempts various escapes.

Katame no Kata pairs from Japan and Russia.

Ju no Kata was invented in 1887 to develop strength, balance, and flexibility in female judo neophytes. This kata sometimes resembles paired gymnastics because the players move in graceful cooperation without throws or falls, rather than in attack and defense sequences. Even today, women often fill the *Ju no Kata* teams at competitions, but senior male judo players are required to demonstrate proficiency as well. Three of the ten teams were male, including one from the U.S., and the eventual third place Spanish team.

Nage no Kata judges during a break in the action (left to right):
Michael Job (S. Africa), Miguel A. Russo (Argentina), Shoji Sugiyama (Italy), Koshi Onozawa (Japan), and Toshiro Daigo (Japan).

Left: Ju no Kata team of Heiko Rommelmann (l.) and Jeff Giunta (USA) perform before judges from Japan, Belgium, U.S., and Syria. Right: Ju no Kata winning team of Estuko Yokoyama and Chigusa Omori (Japan).

Regardless of the kata, proficiency at this level of competition does not come easily. The Japanese *Nage no Kata* winners of the 2007 Kodokan All-Japan Kata Competition practiced together two hours a day for months in their police gym before the competition. Also, competent kata instruction can often be difficult to find; Mr. Heiko Rommelmann and Mr. Jeff Giunta, senior Pan-Am Judo Union competitors, and the sole U.S. pair in the *Ju no Kata* competition, described their difficulty in finding kata instruction: for years they drove hours one way to practice with their instructor, Mr. Tony Owed (now deceased) of Toledo, Ohio. As in previous Japanese national competitions, the Japanese police had a very strong showing; the police, particularly the Tokyo Metropolitan Police, have very strong judo training and kata programs.

In the end, the Japanese teams swept both first and second in all four events, and the Spanish teams took third in all four events; the Italian teams all placed very highly, too. Italian teams won the secretary general's prize.

There seemed to be little controversy despite the Japanese teams sweeping all top eight positions; the level of competition in Japan is clearly very high and very competitive, and Italy and Spain have dominated European kata competitions. The results did of course engender discussion of the relative levels of kata instruction in Japan, Europe, and the rest of the world, but plenty of foreign players vowed to study hard and return to do better. Some competitors praised the administration afterward, saying it was the best-organized tournament they had ever attended. Several of the foreign players had studied at the Kodokan or at overseas Kodokan seminars in preparation; the two Laotian teams studied there for days immediately prior to the event, and had made remarkable progress, according to one of their training partners.

In a post-competition interview, the *Nage no Kata* team of Toshimitsu Takahashi and Fumikazu Yoda described how they had focused on competition early in their judo careers, but came to believe that understanding the katas was key to their further development as well-rounded judoka and competitors. Policemen from Nagano City on the western side of Honshu, they started kata practice in the fall of 2006 and spent hours a day studying *Nage no Kata*. Their practice ended in a top three finish at the All-Japan competition, and second place in this first global competition.

Kodokan Museum Curator Naoki Murata, the general secretary of the event, and a judo 7th-dan, said in his closing address that while the katas' primary purpose is physical education and combat skills, certain katas were practiced primarily as cultural studies of judo's ancient jujutsu roots. In a later interview, he said that the main purpose of the competition was to highlight the katas' role in judo. Randori is now overly emphasized in judo training, he said, and this tournament is part of an effort by the Kodokan to return kata training to its proper place of importance. Unfortunately, because of the preparation required for the judo events in the upcoming Beijing 2008 Olympics and the need to have the All-Japan Judo Kata Competition in 2008, the Kodokan does not plan an international event in 2008, but perhaps in 2009.

Asked to comment on rumors that Japan may try to get acceptance of judo katas as an Olympic event, perhaps in time for Tokyo's bid to host the 2016 Summer Games, Mr. Murata noted that the trend in the Olympics has been to reduce judo events, not increase them, since the inclusion of women's events doubled the number of judo events. He also cited the success of the Pan-American and European Judo Unions' kata competitions, and said that the Kodokan leadership hopes that the other regional judo unions, the Asian, Oceania, and African Judo Unions, will take the lead in fostering interest in the katas through more instruction and competition. The Kodokan supports such efforts, he said, and hopes to help foster technical kata instruction worldwide.

To that end, there was an extensive kata seminar for international judges and participants after the competition, led by the Kodokan's chief instructor, Toshiro Daigo, one of the world's most famous judoka and one of only seventeen 10th-dans, the highest rank in judo. He provided detailed insights into the katas' historic origins and the principles behind each move in an effort to increase the general level of competence.

By preserving and demonstrating the ancient jujutsu techniques and practical applications of judo, the practice of katas and events like the First Kodokan Judo Kata International Tournament provide great insights into the heritage of this modern, global martial art.

Bibliography

Kano, J. (1986). *Kodokan Judo*. Tokyo: Kodansha.

Kodokan. *Kodokan judo kata series*. Tokyo: Kodokan, various years. The Kodokan recently published a series of small, introductory books for each kata, but only in Japanese. See http://www.hint.co.jp/cgi-bin/kshop/kshop_j.pl/page=book_fr_j.html

Kotani, S. and Otaki, T. (1971). *Judo no kata: Zen*. (*Judo kata: Complete*.) Tokyo: Fumaido.

Mifune, K. (2004). *The canon of judo: Classic teachings on principles and techniques*. Tokyo: Kodansha International.

Otaki, T., and Draeger, D. (1983). *Judo formal techniques: A complete guide to Kodokan randori no kata*. Tokyo: Tuttle.

Shinagawa Judo Association (1984). *Miru, manabu, oshieru: Irasu judo no lata* (*See, learn, teach: Illustrated judo kata*). Tokyo: Shinagawa Judo Association.

chapter 5

The Way of Kata in Kodokan Judo

by Llyr C. Jones, Ph.D., and Michael J. Hanon, Ph.D.

Illustrations courtesy of Carl DeCrée, except where noted.

Introduction

In an article De Crée and Jones (2009) explain how Kodokan[1] Judo, developed by Kano Jigoro (1860-1938), is an all-around cooperative education, teaching system (pedagogy), and philosophy—based, among other things, on neo-Confucianist values, traditional school Japanese martial arts, and modern Western educational principles. In particular, judo emphasizes the holistic educational value of training in attack and defense, so that it can be a "path," or way of life, that all people can participate in and draw benefit from. In this way, and contrary to popular debate judo is neither a "martial art" nor a "combat sport."

> [J]udo in the larger sense aims to transcend the sporting context and ... include aspects related to education, health and both physical and emotional self-defense. – Gutiérrez Garcia, Pérez Gutiérrez and Svinth (2010: 127)

The most complete definition of judo available in the literature is that due to Oda Join[2] (1929). Therein, he uses and builds on an original quote by Kano Jigoro that featured in the Kodokan periodical *Judo* (Kano, 1915). Oda writes: "Judo is the most effective way to use the power of the mind and body. Its training cultivates the body and spirit through the practice of attack and defense; the essence of this principled moral code (or "path") is learning through self-awareness. Therefore, judo was innovated so that the ultimate objective is to perfect oneself and benefit from life. In summary, judo is the most effective way of using the mind and body for the benefit of oneself and others" (Oda, 1929: 8).

Kano Jigoro expressed judo's core concepts via the sayings "good use of mind and body" and "mutual welfare and benefit." A spirit of generosity and mutual assistance is therefore integral to judo. Kano envisaged that through the application of judo principles to everyday life a judoist achieves balance and self-mastery, thereby becoming better enabled to deal with routine stresses and to interact with other human beings in positive and mutually beneficial ways.

On the Techniques of Judo

The physical aspects of judo's techniques are based primarily on the Tenjin Shin'yo-ryu, Kito-ryu, and Yoshin-ryu styles of traditional school jujutsu. However, as already explained, the most significant aspect of judo is its blend of physical and mental education to help its practitioners develop well-balanced bodies and minds that will, through a spirit of generosity and mutual assistance, act to improve society as a whole. As such, the techniques of judo are only vehicles to greater goals. They themselves are not the goal. The techniques in judo are actually only of use as a tool to enable a judo practitioner to realize these greater ambitions.

The Elements of Judo Instruction

Writing in the journal *Kokushi* during the early years of the Kodokan's inception, Kano (1899) explains how judo instruction had four components:

- **Free Practice (*randori*):** Practice sparring sessions in which both participants practice attacking and defending, using freely applied throwing and/or pinning techniques (Kawamura and Daigo, 2000: 109–110).
- **Forms (*katas*):** Formal movement pattern exercises containing idealized model movements illustrating specific combative principles (Ibid: 86).
- **Lectures (*kogi*):** Lectures on judo principles were viewed as an essential part of judo education. Kano believed that training for matches or combat was enhanced greatly by teaching theory via lectures.
- **Dialogue (*mondo*):** "Question / answer" sessions between students and teachers were also considered important to reinforce the practical and formal learning.

Murata Naoki, the present curator of the Kodokan museum and library, adds contest (*shiai*) to this list, stating that contest is an important supplementary component of the judo learning process (Murata, 2007).

It is also important to recognize that the way of teaching judo outlined above was actually never implemented beyond Japan. A notable exception, though, was Trevor Leggett's (1914-2000) two-hour, invitation-only Sunday class at the Budokwai, London. Hoare (2000) writes how those sessions "were always packed," with the class itself "being a mixture of grinding hard work, contest and instruction on every aspect of judo." Similarly, Hicks (1996) recalls that for Leggett "judo was an ethical and educational training which opened doors of understanding far beyond the dojo," and how even "his most dedicated pupils were sometimes alarmed when required to write essays."

Why was no tradition of formal judo education through lectures and dialogue ever established and embedded on a wide-scale basis outside of Japan? In judo's formative years it was Kano himself and other senior teachers who directed the lectures and dialogue. Despite Kano and the other seniors undertaking considerable international travel, they were primarily resident in Japan. With only very limited exceptions, teachers of comparable knowledge who could lead formal learning simply did not exist elsewhere. For this reason, no such instructional practice was established.

Furthermore, with the continued internationalization of judo and the International Judo Federation's (IJF) ever-increasing emphasis on sports competition, even the practice of kata became marginalized and viewed as a historical oddity. This left behind a pared-down and distorted judo consisting of only free practice and contest, which is today what most judo practitioners think of as being the totality of judo.

Kata Practice in Current Times

In the article "Competition, Kata and the Art of Judo" (Jones, 2005) it was explained how the practice of the kata in judo had become deemphasized. In his article Jones outlined how the IJF's and national governing bodies' (NGB) emphasis on the sports-competitive aspects of judo and winning medals had produced generations of fighters and coaches who believed that kata practice was outdated and had no relevance or value.

Jones's views were later echoed by Alessio Oltremari in an online article: "Competition and fighting has enchanted generations of judo practitioners and, through applying principles from several sports to judo, they have forgotten its origins and meaning. The important thing is to win—never mind if the technique used is dirty, vulgar and dangerous …. Although technique is absent it does not matter when brute force is enough to achieve the win. Better to be weight training rather than wasting time on deepening technique" (Oltremari, n.d.).

In recent years however, there has been a resurgence in the popularity of kata—one driven not by an appreciation of the self-improvement that accrues from regular kata practice, but by the medal-winning opportunities provided by the rapidly expanding phenomenon of "kata championships." Indeed, such is the growing popularity of kata as a competitive pursuit that the development of training strategies for achieving success in kata championships is starting to feature as a research topic, for example, see Sheedy (2010).

THE KATAS OF KODOKAN JUDO

Kata as a Living Textbook

Kata practice is an important training method in most modern and traditional Japanese martial arts. Finn (1991: 211) is particularly insightful, writing that katas are "prearranged forms[3] in Japanese martial arts that are like a living text book. They contain all the fundamental information in animate form, with which to perfect technique and understanding of the particular skill."

The Listed Katas

There exist ten "listed"[4] Kodokan katas (De Crée and Jones, 2009). This is despite several popular sources incorrectly claiming that there would be only seven, eight, or nine official Kodokan katas. The ten katas are detailed in Table 1, which itself is structured based on how the katas are commonly categorized according to purpose (Kotani, Osawa, and Hirose, 1968: 1; Otaki and Draeger, 1983: 32-33).

In his opening lecture to the 2008 Kodokan Summer Kata Course, Daigo Toshiro[5] gave a brief overview with some history of each currently practiced and recognized kata, listing nine distinct katas overall (Kano, n.d., in Daigo, 2008; Kotani and Otaki, n.d., in Daigo, 2008-2009). Daigo's lecture subsequently formed the basis of his broad multi-part article on kata which was serialized in seven parts in the Kodokan's periodical, *Judo* (Daigo, 2008-2009).

In counting nine Kodokan katas, Daigo inexplicably omits the female self-defense kata, *Joshi Goshin Ho*, which is an officially approved but uncommon Kodokan kata. Additionally, such counting of Kodokan kata ignores both the "Forms of Decision" (*Kime Shiki*) and the "Forms of Gentleness" (*Ju Shiki*), two katas which were considered separately in the past, but today are regarded as being part of the *Sei-ryoku-zen'yo Kokumin-Taiiku*. There also exist several non-Kodokan approved katas of both Japanese and non-Japanese origin. This chapter will not consider any of these unapproved katas.

It is beyond the scope of this chapter to present the technical ("how to") details of the ten Kodokan katas. Full technical details on eight of the ten katas (the two omissions being the *Joshi Goshin Ho* and the *Go-no-kata*) are provided

Table 1: The Katas of Kodokan Judo	
FORMS OF FREE PRACTICE	RANDORI-NO-KATA
- Forms of Throwing	- Nage-no-kata
- Forms of Grappling or Holding	- Katame-no-kata
FORMS OF SELF-DEFENSE	SHOBU-NO-KATA
- Forms of Decisiveness	- Kime-no-kata
- Kodokan Forms of Self-Defense	- Kodokan Goshin-jutsu
- Methods of Self-Defense for Women	- Joshi Goshin Ho
FORMS OF PHYSICAL EDUCATION	RENTAI-NO-KATA
- Forms of Gentleness & Flexibility	- Ju-no-kata
- Forms of (proper use of) Force	- Go-no-kata
- National Physical Education according to (the principle of) best use of energy	- Sei-ryoku-zen'yo Kokumin-Taiiku
FORMS OF THEORY	RI-NO-KATA
- The Five Forms	- Itsutsu-no-kata
- The Antique Forms	- Koshiki-no-kata

in the book *Kodokan Judo*[6] (Kano, 1986: 145-251). For the technical details of the Joshi Goshin Ho, the reader is directed to the text *Kata of Kodokan Judo* (Kotani et al, 1968: 124-153). Similarly, for the technical details of the *Go-no-kata*, the reader is directed to a recent booklet by Mori (2008).

The Purpose of Kata Practice in Judo

In the early days of the Kodokan, Kano Jigoro's teaching method was to start the students off on free practice and allow them to assimilate katas naturally. However, this approach quickly became unsustainable.

Writing in the Kodokan periodical *Sakko* ("Awakening") in 1927, Kano Jigoro explained how katas were created as a teaching framework in response to the fact that the Kodokan was expanding rapidly, and that he (Kano) could not deliver his syllabus just by himself and there were no trained instructors. Kano wrote: "The main reason why the kata[s] were created was because of the ever increasing number of students at the Kodokan. It became impossible to teach students individually as had been the case in the early days, and a system to teach … many students simultaneously was required" (Kano, 1927).

It is a wrong, but widely held, belief that the objective of kata practice in judo is the development of technical refinement and the perfection of technique.[7] This is only a minor component of kata practice, since technique can be perfected in other ways. Proper kata study contributes to improving one's understanding[8] of judo and, as part of this learning, one needs to equate the "perfection of technique" with "perfection of oneself" (Otaki and Draeger, 1983: 35-46, 58-61).

All of the Kodokan katas reflect an ideal goal of judo—"good use of mind and body"—through transmitting the concepts of proper action/reaction, exploiting a moment of opportunity (*debana*), balance breaking (*kuzushi*), and "remaining mind" (*zanshin*). Additionally, each Kodokan kata makes a specific contribution to teaching different inherent judo principles and aspects of control—for example, control of breathing, control of posture and balance, control of speed, control of body movement (*tai-sabaki*), timing, and ultimately emotional control. Even the *Koshiki-no-kata* and the *Itsutsu-no-kata*, katas that seem in first instance to be very remote from everyday judo, are valuable. The understanding that can be derived from their proper practice importantly contributes to the development of "inner feeling" (*kimochi*), a "sense of balance breaking, and a "sense of positioning and set-up" (*tsukuri*).

In the book *Judo* marking the centenary of Kano Jigoro's birth, Kodokan officials stated: "Each ... kata, while demonstrating a number of classical movements, possesses a deep significance. The more kata is practiced the stronger is the feeling that they are a cultural asset embodying the essence of Judo" (Kodokan, 1961: 65).

Looking Deeper into the Kodokan Katas

Each Kodokan kata has its own subliminal thread or theme running through it. However, when one first starts to learn any particular kata, it is usually just its superficial mechanical movements that are learned. Indeed, it is only after much practice and self-exploration that the kata's pervading principles and themes as they apply to judo practice as a whole become revealed. The following pages will look deeper into each of the Kodokan katas to facilitate the development of their more detailed understanding.

Forms of Free Practice

Together, the *Nage-no-kata* and the *Katame-no-kata* are known as the *Randori-no-kata* (forms of free practice). They provide a framework that facilitates the development of free practice skills, and it is essential that they are practiced with the attitude that one would bring to free practice, i.e., gusto and commitment and certainly no "theatrical pretence."

It will now be explained how the learning extractable from the Nage-no-kata transcends that of merely developing skills in throwing techniques. For this purpose the first set of the kata, namely "hand techniques," will be considered. The sequence of techniques is "floating drop," followed by "back-carry throw," followed by "shoulder wheel" (*uki-otoshi* → *seoi-nage* → *kata-guruma*).

For the benefit of further explanation, it is now appropriate to introduce two terms common to judo: *tori* and *uke*. During controlled practice, tori is the person who applies a throw or another technique. Uke is the person who receives the technique.

- **Floating drop (*uki-otoshi*):** When uke attacks tori he does so with all his might regardless of his situation and is thrown with a floating drop. Uke never again attacks tori in such an unchecked manner and learns from each failed attack. Moreover, tori adapts to each new attack.
- **Back-carry throw (*seoi-nage*):** Next, uke attacks tori with an explosive, downward forceful blow to the top of the head. Tori repositions his body and directs that force away from his head and down to the ground, using a back-carry throw. As such tori allows uke to throw himself over tori's body, using his (uke's) own force and strength. There is no block; tori merely turns then throws. The purpose of this technique is to demonstrate a key principle in judo (that of nonresistance) with uke being undone by the force of his own attack. Tori does not throw in the conventional sense of the word, but merely utilizes uke's own action to defeat him. "Maximum efficiency with minimum effort."
- **Shoulder wheel (*kata-guruma*):** Uke attacks again, but this time keeps his body rigid and stiff to avoid the throwing responses he has already received. Once again, though, uke is overcome by the understanding of tori who throws him with a shoulder wheel.

This pattern repeats itself across the entire kata. In the complete Nage-no-kata, uke will attack tori fifteen times, and each time tori will neutralize that attack and use the force or action of uke's own attack to prevail. Therefore, as tori progresses with the study of Nage-no-kata, he develops insight into basic and complex biomechanics, in particular how to apply himself to overcome the actions of an attacking uke. Tori also learns good technique and in doing so becomes able to cross-reference this learning with that from free practice. Finally, tori learns how his own body and mind react under physical and psychological stress, and also how to adapt to a given situation utilizing both his body and his mind in an effective and productive manner.

The Katame-no-kata is concerned with learning control, in particular, how tori can best use his body in an efficient manner to control uke on the ground. Tori must work on his versatility and show excellent body movement while grappling, and uke must strive to escape and exploit any weaknesses in tori's techniques. Moreover, each and every time the Katame-no-kata is practiced, uke should continue to test tori by looking for his weak points and then attacking them. Similarly, tori should find new ways of nullifying uke's new escape attempts. Both tori and uke should assimilate this learning from the Katame-no-kata and leverage it for the benefit of their free practice and contest efforts.

Forms of Self-Defense

The *Kime-no-kata*, the *Kodokan Goshin-jutsu*, and the *Joshi Goshin Ho* are classified as *Shobu-no-kata* (forms of self-defense). These katas reflect what is crucial when involved in a "real" fight to the death (*shinken shobu*), where the central objective is to defeat an adversary and survive. They teach effective body movement, speed, coordination, and control of posture while controlling another person, irrespective of the particular technique or kata being studied.

Forms of Physical Education

The *Ju-no-kata*, the *Go-no-kata* and the *Sei-ryoku-Zen'yo Kokumin-Taiiku* are grouped together as *Rentai-no-kata* (forms of physical education), where the foremost objective is to educate the body to remain healthy. In particular, the Ju-no-kata teaches the principles of resistance and non-resistance, flexibility, and suppleness; the Go-no-kata teaches the principle of the appropriate use of controlled force and develops physical conditioning; and the Sei-ryoku-Zen'yo Kokumin-Taiiku builds up physical development and coordination, as well as laying a foundation for the development of basic judo skills.

The Ju-no-kata does not teach "fighting techniques" in any conventional sense or with the idea of literally using those techniques in combat. Rather, the Ju-no-kata includes a number of attacks and defenses to demonstrate the efficient redirection of force and movement. In addition, as neither tori nor uke is thrown or held down during the course of the kata, it can be practiced anywhere by anyone, even those who are old or nervous. The Ju-no-kata conveys the principle of not countering force with force; it teaches how to respond to action with a reaction that instead of force (*go*) is yielding (*ju*). Uke attacks tori and tori neutralizes that attack, using the attack itself to prevail. For this reason, those who practice the Ju-no-kata merely as fifteen physical movements are missing the purpose of the kata. While the physical element of the kata provides vital lessons in the application of yielding, the Ju-no-kata is actually a set of exercises in tori controlling his mind and emotions to find inner harmony and then blending that harmony with uke. The Ju-no-kata is aptly named and is regarded by many as the finest of all the Kodokan katas.

The Go-no-kata provides a framework for the correct learning of the basics of judo without throwing. It teaches tori to use force effectively, without ever relying on force as the primary means to overcome uke. Additionally, the Go-no-kata teaches the precision use of one's body, especially how to use both focused strength and yielding at critical timings during judo techniques. The Go-no-kata also assists in the development of physical strength itself and contributes to increased willpower and "spiritual energy" in the sense of "a healthy spirit in a healthy body" (De Crée and Jones, 2009).

Both the Ju-no-kata and the Go-no-kata convey the meaning of *ju-no-ri*, i.e., the core principle of jujutsu whereby one avoids opposing an opponent's force and power directly in favor of using it to one's advantage. They also accord with a core principle of judo, which can be expressed in a number of ways: "softness overcomes hardness," "flexibility overcomes stiffness," "gentleness controls strength," or "win by yielding" (Ibid).

The Sei-ryoku-Zen'yo Kokumin-Taiiku is not a strict kata, but rather a physical education exercise[9] that may be practiced in a very informal manner with considerable degrees of freedom. (Note also that the word "kata" does not even feature in the name, reflecting that it is even freer in nature than a series labeled *ho* or "method.") It is divided into two main types of exercise: solo practice (*tandoku renshu*) and partnered practice (*sotai renshu*).

The solo exercises have strikes and kicks, as well as a number of other exercises designed to build muscle tone and harmoniously develop a balanced physique. Most typically, every movement is repeated five times, left and right, before moving on to the next. However, freedom exists to increase the number of repetitions, should it be desired.

The partnered exercises are divided into two main groups: *Kime Shiki* (forms of decision) and *Ju Shiki* (forms of gentleness). The Kime Shiki techniques contain simple versions of several techniques found in the Kime-no-kata including grabs, blows, and attacks with weapons. The Ju Shiki section has two groups of five techniques each, taken directly from the Ju-no-kata.

Forms of Theory

The *Itsutsu-no-kata* and the *Koshiki-no-kata* are grouped together as Ri-no-kata (forms of theory). Both of these katas are rooted in traditional school jujutsu and convey principles from their historical schools of origin. It should, though, be noted that these principles are totally unknown to most people;[10] however, some concepts, such as an "immovable mind" (*fudoshin*), are somewhat known.

The Itsutsu-no-kata expresses the principles of attack and defense in movements evocative of natural phenomena and can be regarded as a physical manifestation of the "philosophical mind" of judo. Discussing the Itsutsu-no-kata in the publication *Judo* (1961), Kodokan officials stated: "It is an artistic and meaningful kata calling for natural movements (the movement of water, the movement of heavenly bodies etc.) to be skillfully expressed by the human body" (Kodokan, 1961: 67).

In this sense, the Itsutsu-no-kata can be considered the kata of "motional principles," a sort of "judo-physics." While the Itsutsu-no-kata is officially attributed to Kano Jigoro (Kano, 1986), recent research by De Crée (2010) indicates that it was not created by Kano, and that it clearly existed in Tenjin Shin'yo-ryu jujutsu under the name "Five Step Oral Teachings" (*Kuden Gohon*).

The Koshiki-no-kata was placed in the Kodokan repertoire as a reminder of judo's heritage being partially in Kito-ryu jujutsu, in particular its Takenaka-ha style (Ibid). Accordingly, the Koshiki-no-kata is also known as the *Kito Kata* and can be thought of as the kata of "judo tradition" or "judo history."

According to the Kodokan (1961) the first movement of the Koshiki-no-kata, the "ready posture" (*tai*), is the basis of the entire kata: "*Tai* is the basis of the Kito Kata. It teaches that it is important to adopt a calm posture; to quiet the spirit; to clear the mind and, by these means, to discern the opponent's strength and weaknesses. So the original object of the *Koshiki-no-kata* was to teach not so much technique as methods of training the mind" (Kodokan, 1961: 69).

The core purpose of the Ri-no-kata is to develop a higher understanding of the fundamental and deeper "essence" and perhaps even "esoteric" principles of judo (De Crée and Jones, 2009). The Ri-no-kata involve the mental state of the attacker, and the principles of physics, anticipation, and reaction. They require developing an understanding of the mental state of the attacker at the point of attack ("What is he trying to accomplish?" and "How does one anticipate the attack?"), and what laws of physics and principles of yielding should one apply to that situation. These are very complex ideas, and it is the synthesis and compression of all those concepts into individual katas that make the Itsutsu-no-kata and the Koshiki-no-kata so difficult and beyond the comprehension of most judo practitioners at any given point in their judo career.

The *Ri-no-kata* are therefore the logical final stage of the kata-learning process. They cannot be properly studied until the Randori-no-kata, the Shobu-no-kata, and the Rentai-no-kata have all been mastered.

Inner Feeling

It has already been explained how kata in judo involves the synthesis of a whole group of physical and mental concepts and disciplines in the performance of extremely challenging routines and exercises, and how this makes the kata study a complete education in itself. "The concept of kata is often misunderstood. Although various techniques are executed, kata should not be considered a catalog of designated responses to specific dangerous situations. Rather, kata is a method of transmitting core principles and concepts" (Cunningham, 2008: 10).

Katas, therefore, are about inner feeling (*kimochi*) and are as much about training the mind as the body. If katas are performed as "mere movements" then these educational aspects are missed.

Kata, Intrinsic Energy, and No-Mindness

Guy Pelletier, the world's highest Kodokan ranked judo practitioner of non-Japanese descent (Kodokan eighth-degree rank), considers the relationship of kata, intrinsic energy (*ki*), and "no-mindness" (*mushin*), writing:

> A good kata is more than just a number of physically correct actions. It is the mental attitude of the two partners who realize the kiai, or concentration of spirit. Therein lies the essence of kata. The flow of mental energy is very noticeable when attending a quality demonstration.
>
> Uke, like tori, must show their "ki" or mental energy. Their external attitude is one of calm, quiet vigilance and self-confidence. You and your partner's ki unite and rely on kiai, which in turn induces a mental state called *Muga-mushin*. This however is not attained until after much

experience. *Muga-mushin* means "no self, no mind." It is a state of indifference that frees the consciousness of the actions undertaken. In this state, the spirit solves problems automatically, so to speak, hence its importance in self-defence and judo.

Kata is the best way for a [judo practitioner] to do judo in a state of ignorance of the specific actions he is doing. A [judo practitioner] is an expert when he reaches this stage. Kata refines the spirit, enabling him to carry out actions faster than through itself, in this way the art becomes an "art without art." – Pelletier, n.d.

Protect, Break, Separate

Shu-ha-ri is an educational concept rooted in the martial arts and other classical Japanese disciplines, such as flower arranging, puppetry, theater, poetry, painting, sculpture, and weaving. According to Takamura (1986), it has been instrumental in the survival of many of these older knowledge traditions. Shu-ha-ri describes the learning curve to mastery through the stages of "protect" (imitation/absorbing,) "break" (understanding/detaching/digressing), and "separating" (consolidation/transcending the physical).

Using a lecture note by Ukichi, Daigo (2008) explained how one progresses from the basic form through to a deep understanding of kata using this concept:

Shu — First stage (protect): The stage of shu consists in studying a teacher's lesson correctly. The teaching of a particular school must be studied faithfully without any change. This is the stage of imitation. In short, it is the way to preserve and protect the integrity and the dignity of a school. This is the stage of shu.

Ha — Second stage (break): After progressing more after repetitive kata practice, a student begins to question and discover by himself. He separates from his master and inquires beyond the superficial instruction of kata movements. After, self-individuality is harnessed. The width of the style is expanded. The meaning of kata is investgated deeply. This is a stage of ha.

Ri — Third stage (separate): Furthermore, kata practice is treated freely and spontaneously. It is in the realm of the new creation which is made by oneself. This is a stage of ri.

– Ukichi, n.d., in Daigo, 2008

Further insight into the application of shu-ha-ri to kata study in the martial arts is provided by Takamura (1986) and Klens-Bigman (n.d.). The material presented therein is as relevant to judo as it is to the specific arts considered in the articles themselves.

Harmony, Concentration, Immersion, and Purity

In a personal communication with the authors, the noted judo practitioner Paul Nogaki (sixth-degree rank) recalled the teachings that he received from Daigo in 1980 regarding the thought process that one should strive to achieve when practicing kata. He stated that "kata in judo is about learning mental and physical discipline, and connecting the two together in attempting extremely difficult routines and exercises. Even the words to describe the ultimate goals to be attained in kata—*in'yo-wago*, *senshin*, *seiboku*, and *genshitsu*—are really almost impossible to translate correctly into another language [other than Japanese]" (Nogaki, 2009).

Both Nogaki (2009) and De Crée (2009) kindly provided translations of the concepts introduced by Daigo to explain the ultimate goal of "kata Nirvana."

- ***In'yo-wago:*** In'yo-wago means a harmony or balance between yin and yang energies[11] (and what they mean in the martial arts) leading to strength. This concept no doubt originates from Kito-ryu and not from judo. Obtaining this yin/yang balance is a lengthy process, and not one that judo consciously discusses or tackles. Arguably, it is something that is the goal of the Ri-no-kata, although practicing other katas could also help.

- ***Senshin:*** Senshin literally means "committed," "undivided attention" or "concentration"—important components in the development of spiritual power. However, in judo, the concept of ki is not cultivated in that sense, though Kano Jigoro used and talked about *sei-ryoku* or "optimization," which is the equivalent. (This was a conscious choice, in order to demystify ki). For Kano, sei-ryoku existed in two components: a physical component (*chikara*), and a spiritual component (without such being some mystical superior power). Using the two in harmony (as per in'yo-wago) resulted in "optimization," often known in judo as "efficient (or best) use of energy."

- ***Genshitsu:*** Genshitsu literally means "commitment." This can be extrapolated to mean "total immersion."

- ***Seiboku:*** Seiboku means "to be gentle and pure" and thus different from powerful, abrupt judo. The purity refers to proper technique and use of balance breaking, timing, and setup. If so, then no force is necessary, much like Mifune Kyuzo's "empty jacket" judo.[12]

The above is a key original contribution of this chapter, as the authors are unaware of any other written sources that present this insight. Additionally, they are unaware of any sources where the concepts discussed are related to kata practice.

THE KATA CHAMPIONSHIPS AND
THE SPORTIFICATION OF KATA

Under this heading, a critical evaluation of the impact that the "sportification" of kata is having upon this important element of judo is presented. In doing so, the questions posed by Oltremari (n.d.) will be indirectly answered: "Can the exercise of kata in judo be considered a sport? Can the performance of an exercise in judo forms be likened to an exercise in gymnastics" (Oltremari, n.d.)?

History

Kata championships are not new. The British Judo Association (BJA) held its first National Kata Championship (together with the first British Veterans Championship) at Woolwich College in London in 1981. Recent years, however, have seen a marked increase in the number and level of kata championships, and events now regularly take place at regional, national, continental, and world levels.

At the continental level, for example, the first European Kata Championships were hosted by the BJA and held in Burgess Hill, Sussex, in 2005. (A European Masters [veterans] Championship was also held at the same time.) The proceedings were attended by Daigo from the Kodokan and dominated by kata pairs from Italy. Subsequent European Kata Championships have been held under the auspices of the European Judo Union (EJU) in Italy (2006), Germany (2007), Malta (2008), and Romania (2009). Other Continental associations have also organized their own kata championships.

At the world level, championships have been organized since 1999 by the World Masters Judo Association (WMJA). The WMJA is an entity founded in Ottawa, Canada, in 1998 with the purpose of encouraging participation in competition judo and kata for judo practitioners aged thirty years plus, in a fun, friendly, and family-orientated manner. The first such event was held in Welland, Canada. Subsequent WMJA kata (and contest) championships have been held in Canada (2000), the United States (2001), UK (2002), Japan (2004), Canada (2005), France (2006), Brazil (2007), Belgium (2008), and the United States (2009).

The IJF itself was somewhat slow off the mark in organizing kata championships, with the first IJF event, known as the Kata World Cup, taking place in Paris, France, in November 2008, the event essentially being a rehearsal for the first official IJF Kata World Championships that were held in October 2009 in Valetta, Malta. The second such IJF event was held in Budapest, Hungary, in May 2010.

In parallel to organizing its own masters' event, the IJF discharged additional actions that could be interpreted as a conscious effort to marginalize and smother the efforts of the WMJA.[13] In 2009, the WMJA finally gave in to the inevitable and agreed to disband itself in 2010. The final WMJA event was held in Montreal, Canada, in August 2010, after which sole organizational control of world-level masters judo passed to the IJF. It is only the passage of time that will reveal whether the IJF will be able to preserve the spirit of masters judo as originally intended and established by the WMJA.

The first Kodokan Judo Kata International Tournament championships, organized under the joint auspices of the Kodokan Judo Institute and the All Japan Judo Federation, took place in October 2007 at the Kodokan Judo Institute in Tokyo. This significant event is described by Gatling (2008).

Kata Championships: The Positive

It is clear that the introduction of a competitive element has provided the competitive judo player with a source of motivation for studying katas, i.e., the tangible goal of a medal. It should also be stated that some of the kata performances achieved in kata competition are outstanding in all respects, particularly those by judo practitioners from Italy, Japan, and Spain. Such spirited performances though are often the exception to the rule.

It is also clear that as a direct consequence of kata championships, there are currently more judo practitioners aware of and practicing katas than at any time in the recent past. Without this competition-led revival, there is a high probability that kata practice would have silently and progressively vanished from judo, leaving behind only the undignified and increasingly commercialized "jacketed wrestling sport" that the IJF has made judo into.

Given the above, it is often remarked, "Without kata championships, kata would be dead." This chapter will now argue that due to the values and constraints imposed by kata championships, kata as the learning aid envisaged by Kano Jigoro is already "near death." Oltremari (n.d.) writes: "The same barbarism that has pervaded *shiai* [contest] and turned it into an inferno conducted in a pit in an arena is about to break forth on kata. A new gymnasium for the triumph of the ego is about to rise, while a scheme [kata] created for completely different purposes slowly disappears .... The introduction of the principles of modern sport in this discipline [kata] will distort its essence and meaning, first condemning it to its cultural contextualization and then to its very ending" (Oltremari, n.d.).

Kata Championships: The Negative

It will now be explained how kata championships are eroding the underlying benefits and fundamental principles of kata training and why their very concept (i.e., the sportification of an educational tool) should be regarded as being fundamentally flawed.

Kata championships do not accommodate individuality, have no room for interpretation, and rigidly limit any creative endeavor in the performance of any particular kata. They consider only how well the "kata performance"[14] has complied with a given marking scheme, regardless of the impact that this has on the development of the performers as judo practitioners. The impact of this is that in order to achieve success at kata competition, kata practitioners are compelled to train not for enhanced insight or personal growth or to improve their own kata practice, but rather to present "carbon copy" duplicates of the physical movements of the kata as shown in the relevant teaching film. The sole purpose of this charade is to enable kata judges to conduct "like-for-like" evaluations, with the victors being the performers who can demonstrate the best-looking "kata copy" or "kata clone," irrespective of the spirit and realism. By dint of this approach, kata championships focus entirely on the *shu* ("protect") aspect of kata study and pay no respect at all to the *ha* ("separate") or *ri* ("leave") elements.

If the focus of kata practice becomes success at a kata championship rather than self-improvement, then the entire training will become imbalanced due to overemphasizing minor technical aspects and conventions[15] that should not be a source of concern in regular training. By slavishly copying the ritualized movements captured in a teaching film, both the original educational intent of kata practice and the associated holistic learning that results from proper kata practice are being lost. The resulting kata renditions often end up empty and fake, as they are devoid of any meaningful action/reaction component. In reality, katas can never be copied, and all kata performances are, of course, nonrepeatable. This is because no two performing pairs are the same (in terms of physique and psychology), and no two circumstances are ever encountered again, even between the same pair.

Even if one is prepared to accept the principle that kata can be evaluated, the concept of summing the scores of individual techniques in a complete kata to see how one set of performers compares against others and then to award medals (*à la* figure skating or gymnastics) based on this ranking, is unsound. Every kata is a complete representation from its beginning to its end, and any evaluation of a kata must therefore be for the kata as a whole and not the sum of its individual parts.

The absurdity of the "sum of the individual parts" approach to evaluating kata performance can be illustrated by the example of Daigo, who was demonstrating Nage-no-kata at a Kodokan "New Year's rice-cake cutting ceremony" (Otaki and Draeger, 1983: 432). Daigo was the victim of an error of his uke, who attacked with a technique out of sequence and began the third ("rear sacrifice techniques," *ma-sutemi-waza*) set of the kata with a blow, instead of engaging and taking a grip as prescribed for the correct throw in the sequence, the "circle throw" (*tomoe-nage*). Daigo reacted seamlessly and effectively: unable to take the prescribed grip, he simply stepped in and executed the correct, logical response

judo

柔道

"the flexible way"

Illustration courtesy of
www.iStockphoto.com.

to the attack, the "rear throw" (*ura-nage*). He then performed this throw to the left. Thereafter, he executed *tomoe-nage* (as the second set of techniques) and then proceeded to perform the correct third set of techniques. Such was the intensity of Daigo's actions and so well coordinated were his reflexes and reaction that many spectators were totally unaware of what had happened.

Daigo's response was the best one possible in the circumstances and much better than hesitating, pausing completely, or starting again. However, in the context of the Nage-no-kata the overall performance still contained an "error." The question then becomes the consequence of an "error" in kata. In a kata competition, an error such as that made by Daigo's uke would be viewed as being "very poor" and would have resulted (as a minimum) in a zero score (IJF, 2010; 2010a) for that particular technique. In a kata competition this would have meant that they would have had no chance of medaling.

However, when what happened is evaluated in the broader context of judo, the error can be regarded as trivial, it only being an error in the logical progression of the Nage-no-kata. Daigo should have been praised for his flexible mind and for executing an appropriate response against the particular attack. Great judo is not how one performs under benign conditions, but how one performs, acts, and responds under hazardous or unanticipated conditions.

It is particularly disheartening to those wishing to promote the serious study of judo and its katas that as a direct consequence of the current emphasis on competition the true purpose and place of judo kata practice as a learning tool is being lost. Additionally, ignorant and incorrect information on kata is being promulgated, a particularly heinous example being the worthless description of kata proffered by the director of communications and media relations for USA Judo (the NGB for judo in the United States), Nicole Jomantas: "Kata is a forms-based judo discipline in which two athletes perform a set routine of judo techniques which are then scored by a panel of judges" (Jomantas: 2009).

Jomantas' definition reflects the wretched attitude toward kata that permeates contemporary judo, i.e., the obsession of NGBs with the competitive, as opposed to educational, aspects of judo. It is also clear that Jomantas has thought nothing about the logic of her definition, since cursory consideration of the question "If a kata is performed without judges, is it not still a kata?" should have revealed just how flawed it was.

Questioning the Purpose of Kata Practice

Katas were not created to be "judged" or to be studied as an exercise in "how to perform a ceremonial kata demonstration"; rather, they were developed as a living and breathing tool to support the correct learning and practice of judo principles.

Envisaged by Kano, katas were primarily intended as a type of practice. However, when one sees katas today, it is always as a demonstration, and virtually never as a true practice of technique or self-defense, or even simple pre- or post-training exercises. In Kano's time, kata practice need not have been a complete ceremonial performance, but simply an activity to improve one's understanding of judo, or to warm up, or to strengthen one's muscles, or to enhance one's reflexes, flexibility, coordination, and focus, or to really learn how to defend oneself against a certain attack.

When katas are first studied, it is easy to become overinvolved with their ceremony, ritual, and mechanics. Notwithstanding the genuine importance of those aspects, they should not be allowed to detract from the greater lessons of the kata, and to understand those lessons it is necessary for judo practitioners to question and ask "what is a kata?" more deeply and with greater understanding and appreciation. While training for a kata competition will support the learning of the specific technical moves in a kata, it will not, however, lead to an understanding of why one studies katas, the benefits, the intentions of the creators of katas, or the tradition and psychology of kata practice.

Katas should always be studied for their educational content and never just to "look good." Katas belong to every judo practitioner as an individual and cannot be a clone of any other person's. In this way, all kata renditions should be different, and at a fundamental level, for a kata rendition to be "correct," it is only the order of the techniques, the protocol of the kata in question, and the appropriate spirit that are essential to preserve.

Set against the original purpose and intent of kata, it is clear that the only justifiable rationale for kata championships is the opportunity they provide to be critiqued by one's peers and seniors. However, peer and senior feedback should be readily obtainable with any form of competition with others. Indeed, the concept of competing against others in kata performance should be anathema to anyone with even the most rudimentary understanding of Kodokan judo. "How can one possibly compete in an exercise that is about personal development?" "How can one judge one human being against another?" And since judo is the education of the physical and emotional being that one is, "How can such judgments be reached (since one's kata practice is a manifestation of one's judo and thus of oneself)?"

Katas performed well and with understanding can be a thrilling and interesting spectacle for an observer, as well as enjoyable and rewarding for the participants. Mechanistically cloned kata demonstrations are worthless for both participant and observer. As explained earlier, the spirit and mental attitude in a person doing a kata dictate its feel and flow, and this can be about as individual as anything can be in judo. As Damblat writes: "Learning a kata is relatively easy, but knowing a kata is only the first step. The ultimate goal is to discover, to understand or grasp its *raison d'etre* and the message it conveys. One must first assimilate, then feel, and it [the kata] must be alive …. The execution of a kata should never be done mechanically and without soul. It need not be demonstrative, but simply living and logical while demonstrating the governing principles of judo so that the practice is beneficial and contributes to some evolution and understanding of judo …. The aesthetics of a kata must reflect the sincerity of control, specific techniques and a perfect communion of mind of both partners" (Damblat, n.d.: 3).

At this point, the authors will register their disappointment that the Kodokan has condoned and embraced the concept of kata championships. Although Kano Jigoro recognized the value of contest, kata used as a surrogate competition was never part of his thinking. The authors do acknowledge, though, that the Kodokan's motives for doing so were sincere and well intentioned (Kano, 2007):[16]

> We can see today increasing interests in learning kata, not only in Japan but also throughout all the countries of the world. As a result, the 1st Kodokan Judo Kata International Tournament 2007 is being held… I sincerely hope that all judokas will contribute to the development of judo through learning kata.
>
> Most of the competitors and judges participating in this event are totally involved in judo as instructors. I have high expectations that all the participants will take this opportunity to recognize the essence of Kodokan judo anew through kata and promote authentic judo.

Despite its genuine motivation for supporting kata tournaments, it is the Kodokan that is the guardian of Kano Jigoro's legacy, and it should discharge this function in part through the setting and maintenance of appropriate standards. The promotion of kata that is fake, empty, and without action/reaction is not judo, and the concept of competing against others in kata performance is totally contrary to the philosophy and intent of the founder.

In closing this section it is worth noting that perhaps "some light exists at the end of the tunnel," as some serious study is now underway at the Kodokan, which could be interpreted as part of an ongoing effort to address the issue of kata evaluation and perhaps address the recent deteriorations (Murata and Todo, 2007; 2009).

The main purposes of Murata and Todo's work are to research how to develop a simple and clear method of evaluating kata performances, and to make recommendations as to how to modify the present systems. In so doing, they examined the European and Japanese kata evaluation methods with the following findings (Murata and Todo, 2007):

- The European "reduction only" system is not good because it does not recognize positive aspects of performance, only the negative;
- The Japanese system does not allow for differentiation between good and better, or poor and worse kata performances;
- Neither system clarifies the principles to be judged;
- The absence of an official kata championships referee system.

Murata and Todo's formal conclusions were as follows: "Kata techniques exist on rational mechanism of *tsukuri* and *kake*, and this mechanism should be called *Waza no Ri* (principle of techniques). Neither students nor teachers could learn and teach any kata without knowing the Waza no Ri. No judges could evaluate any Kata performance without knowing this Waza no Ri" (Ibid). *Tsukuri* is body positioning in preparation for executing a throw. *Kake* is the finishing or execution of the throw.

Murata and Todo (2009) recently extended their work with a specific focus on the Koshiki-no-kata and this study remains to be evaluated by the authors.

Conclusions

We live in very different times compared to the days and era of Kano Jigoro and, as we become removed further and further from them, our understanding of many of judo's essential aspects becomes less and less. Katas are vital learning tools and to complete one's judo, one needs to learn, practice, and understand them. Moreover, one should also exploit the lessons that kata imparts in both free practice and contest.

An argument could be advanced that the proper teaching and evaluation of kata demand a considerable intellectual level. In today's judo (where belt ranks are largely awarded on the basis of current or past competitive prowess, rather than deep judo knowledge and skill), a nonintellectual high-degree holder has large hierarchical supremacy over a highly intellectual lower grade. This creates problems when it comes to the accurate teaching of katas.

In the main, the judo kata landscape is a wilderness populated with well-intended, but often uninformed, teachers. Accordingly, most kata instruction focuses on the mechanical aspects of kata (movements, timing, and distance), and says nothing about feeling or techniques on how to understand and improve spirit. Frequently this is not strictly the fault of the teachers, as they are often unaware of any deeper purpose behind what they teach, and thus have no knowledge to pass on to their students beyond the superficial physical movements.

What Fraguas (2001) wrote about karate-do is equally true for judo: "Unfortunately, 95 percent of the people don't understand kata, only the outside movements which are irrelevant without understanding" (Fraguas, 2001: 283).

Moreover, as discussed in this chapter, the introduction of kata competitions has only reinforced the emphasis on the mechanics of kata to the virtual exclusion of all their other aspects. Accordingly, a paradoxical situation now exists whereby kata practice is becoming more popular with rank-and-file judo practitioners, but the true purpose and spirit of kata usage is becoming increasingly lost.

If one returns to premodern, i.e., pre-kata competition, ways of doing kata, one does not acquire the form of movement that most judo practitioners seem to think that kata practice entails. Instead, one acquires an exercise that encapsulates judo principles, which, once understood and felt, can be experimented with to any degree of "aliveness" that one wants within the confines of one's training—for example, working with real live blades in the Kime-no-kata and the *Kodokan Go-shin Jutsu*, or wearing traditional armor (*yoroi*) for the Koshiki-no-kata. Such practice and experimentation would produce katas that are very different from the robotic, sequenced forms seen in most contemporary kata competitions.

Studying katas the way they were originally developed is not about learning judo's history; rather, it is about doing judo correctly in the first place. While good teachers produce good judo practitioners, great teachers can help their pupils achieve greatness in life. "Real" kata is one of the tools a "real teacher" uses.

Acknowledgment
The authors would like to thank Professor Carl De Crée and Paul Nogaki for sharing their wisdom and knowledge. The quality of this chapter has been significantly enriched by their many insights and contributions.

Editor's Note
The use of "katas" in this paper to denote the pluralization of "kata" is to conform with the editorial style used in the *Journal of Asian Martial Arts*.

Glossary

Debana	出端		Koryu	古流
Fudoshin	不動心		Kuzushi	崩し
Gendai budo	現代武道		Mushin	無心の心
Genshitsu	言質		Sakk	作興
In'yo-wago	陰陽和合		Seiboku	清穆
Joshi Goshin Ho	女子護身法		Senshin	専心
Kagami Biraki	鏡開き		Shu-ha-ri	守破離
Kata	形		Mushin no shin	無心の心
Ki	気		Tai-sabaki	体捌
Kimochi	気持ち		Tenjin Shin'yo-ryu	天神真楊流
Kito-ryu	起倒流		Tsukuri	作り
Kodokan	講道館		Yoshin-ryu	楊心流
Kokushi	國士		Zanshin	残心

Notes

[1] Kodokan, the headquarters of judo, was originally founded in 1882 by Kano Jigoro, the creator of judo.

[2] Many publications wrongly write Oda's first name as Tsunetane, as opposed to Join.

[3] One of the issues when translating words from one language to another is that subtle meanings and nuances of the original words are often lost. This is very much the case with the word *kata*. Although the accepted translation of kata in judo is "form," other words, such as "template," "pattern," or "style," might be better suited. The word kata is also often used in Japanese culture to describe standard of posture. This is also appropriate.

[4] The term "listed kata" is due to John Cornish (7th-degree judo, 8th-degree aikido) (Cornish, 2004). It refers to formally written sets of choreographed exercises and techniques grouped to illustrate specific principles as opposed to ad hoc prearranged sequences of judo techniques.

[5] Daigo Toshiro (b. 1926) was for many years the chief instructor at the Kodokan Judo Institute. He was promoted to 10th-degree rank in 2006 and is arguably the world's greatest kata expert. See Sidney (2003: 144-153) for a detailed profile of Daigo.

[6] Although Kano Jigoro is presented as the author of this book, it is in fact a compilation by the Kodokan Institute that dates after the founder's death.

7. The practice of any kata, no doubt importantly contributes to developing technical refinement, since to do kata one must be able to "sense" (or "feel") one's partner. It is possible, though, to prevail in free practice and contest without "feeling," by using mainly the elements of surprise, speed, and force. These elements are effective and even important aspects of judo, but they do not represent judo in its entirety. Moreover, they will ultimately fail, as one can always encounter an opponent who is faster and stronger.

8. Here, understanding does not simply mean intellectual understanding, but principle and bodily understanding.

9. Despite Kano's enormous efforts in promoting the Sei-ryoku-Zen'yo Kokumin-Taiiku as a kata of physical exercise, it was not appreciated as much as he wished, partly because of the timing of his death and partly because of the disruption caused by the Second World War.

10. With the exception of some very senior Kodokan teachers, virtually no one, either Japanese or Westerner, is able to completely explain the essence and applicability of the Itsutsu-no-kata and the Koshiki-no-kata and how they integrate with the broader judo syllabus.

11. In Chinese theory, yin and yang: the fundamental principle of two mutually interdependent and constantly interacting polar energies that sustain all living organisms.

12. Mifune Kyuzo (10th-degree rank) was known for the softness of his techniques. He was able to defeat students twice his size while barely seeming to expend any effort. People who trained with him later said, "It was like fighting with an empty jacket."

13. In 2009 the IJF and the EJF refused permission for referees and kata judges to officiate at any WMJA event. Additionally, Budapest, the original planned venue for the WMJA 2009 event, withdrew its candidacy at short notice—allegedly in the face of pressure applied by the IJF.

14. With respect to kata, the oft-used word "performance" is also troublesome to the authors. Performance implies an activity done to entertain or please others. As already explained, kata is done for the benefit and education of the two judo practitioners doing the kata. Any judge who really understands kata should easily be able to differentiate between a pair of judo practitioners genuinely "doing" the kata and a pair who are only "performing" the kata.

15. The IJF has produced a "competition formula" (IJF, 2010; 2010a) that detail how many points to deduct for various categories of "technical errors" in a competitive kata performance. Consequently, when practicing, judo players place much emphasis on avoiding these mistakes at the expense of the overall spirit or realism of the kata.

16. Kano Yukimitsu (b. 1932) is the grandson of Kano Jigoro and was the fourth president of the Kodokan. He stepped down from his post in 2009.

Bibliography

Cunningham, D. (2008). *Samurai weapons: Tools of the warrior.* Tokyo: Tuttle Publishing.

Cornish, J. (Spring 2004). What is kata? *The Bulletin,* 10: 1-2. Available online and from The Kano Society. URL: http://www.kanosociety.org/bulletins/bulletinx10.htm (Retrieved, July 2010).

Daigo, T. (2008). Jigoro Kano, Kodokan Judo-no-kata 1964. Lecture notes from the Kodokan Summer Kata Course. 29 July 2008. Tokyo: Kodokan Judo Institute.

Daigo, T. (2008-2009). Kodokan Judo Kata ni Tsuite (1-7) (About the Kata of Kodokan Judo, Parts 1-7). *Judo,* 79(10): 52-57; 79(11): 7-12; 79(12): 18-23; 80(1): 16-22; 80(2): 43-50; 80(3): 12-16 and 80(4): 3-9. In Japanese.

Damblant, R. (n.d.). Judo—Les katas ou formes: Leur histoire, leure raison d'Être et leurs valeurs (Judo—Kata or forms: Their history, their rationale and their values). Article online and available from Judo Quebec's Website, URL: www.judo-quebec.qc.ca/img/pdf/les_kata_ou_formes.pdf. In French. Retrieved, July 2010.

De Crée, C. (2009). Personal correspondence with Professor Carl De Crée on matters of Japanese-English translation pertaining to the ideals of kata.

De Crée, C. (2010). R*yu-setsu. Judo no musha shugyo–As snow on a willow. A pilgrimage in judo.* Cambridge: Cambridge University Press (In preparation).

De Crée, C. and Jones, L. (2009). Kodokan judo's elusive tenth kata: The Go-no-kata—"Forms of proper use of force," Parts 1-3, *Archives of Budo.* 5, 55-73; 75-82 and 83-95. Articles online and available from the Archives of Budo website, URL:
http://www.archbudo.com/fulltxt.php?ICID=878157 (Part 1)
http://www.archbudo.com/fulltxt.php?ICID=878158 (Part 2)
http://www.archbudo.com/fulltxt.php?ICID=878159 (Part 3)

Finn, M. (1991). *Martial arts: A complete illustrated history.* Leicester: Blitz Editions.

Fraguas, J. (2001). *Karate masters.* Burbank, CA: Unique Publications.

Gatling, L. (2008). The First Kodokan Judo Kata International Competition and its katas. *Journal of Asian Martial Arts,* 17(1), 68-77.

Gutiérrez Garcia, C., Pérez Gutiérrez, M. and Svinth, J. authors (2010). *Judo.* In Green, T. and Svinth, J. editors. (2010). *Martial arts of the world: An encyclopedia of history and innovation,* 1. Santa Barbra: ABC-CLIO.

Hicks, J. (1996). TWOJ Interviewed Trevor Leggett. Article online and available from *The World of Judo* magazine's archives, URL: http:// www.twoj.org/archives/2000/autumn/aut00_news5.html (Retrieved July 2010.) (Originally in: *The world of judo* (1996). Edition No. 6.)

Hoare, S. (2000). Trevor Pryce Leggett 1914-2000. Article online and available from *The World of Judo* magazine's archives, URL: http://www.twoj.org/archives/2000/autumn/aut00_news5.html (Retrieved July 2010.) (Originally in: *The World of Judo* (2000). Edition No. 24.)

International Judo Federation (2010). *World Kata Championships 2010 Budapest, Hungary, Competition Rules*. Budapest: International Judo Federation.

International Judo Federation Data Commission (2010a). *Kata competition 2010*. International Judo Federation.

Jomantas, N. (2009). Team USA to compete at first ever Kata World Championships this weekend (13 October 2009). Article online and available from USA Judo's website, URL: http://judo.teamusa.org/news/article/28266 (Retrieved, July 2010).

Jones, L. (2005). Competition, kata and the art of judo. *Journal of Asian Martial Arts*, 14(3), 72-85.

Kano, J. (n.d.). In Daigo, T. editor. (1964 and 2008). *Kodokan Judo no kata* (The kata of Kodokan judo). Tokyo: Kodokan Publications. Reprinted for the 2008 Kodokan Summer Kata Course. Tokyo: Kodokan Judo Institute.

Kano, J. (1899). Kodokan Judo kogi (Kodokan judo lectures). *Kokushi, 1*(4). (In Japanese.)

Kano, J. (1915). Kodokan Judo gaisetsu (Outline of Kodokan Judo). *Judo. 2*. (In Japanese).

Kano, J. (1927). Kano Jigoro judoka, 12 (Kano Jigoro the judoka, Part 12). *Sakko. 5*(12). (In Japanese).

Kano, J. (1986). *Kodokan judo*. Tokyo: Kodansha International.

Kano, Y. (2007). Welcome Address. *Souvenir Program of the 1st Kodokan Judo Kata International Tournament 2007*. pp. 26–27.

Kawamura, T. and Daigo, T. (Eds.) (2000). *Kodokan new Japanese-English dictionary of judo*. Tokyo: Kodokan Institute.

Klens-Bigman, D. (n.d.). Creativity, bound flow and the concept of shu-ha-ri in kata. Article online and available from FightingArts.com's website, URL: http://fightingarts.com/reading/article.php?id=173 (Retrieved, July 2010).

Kodokan (1957–1999). Qualification for dan promotion. Information online and available from the Kodokan's website, URL: http://www.kodokan.org/e_basic/shoudan.html (Retrieved, June 2010).

Kodokan (1961). *Judo*. Osaka: Nunoi Shobo Co.

Kotani, S., Osawa, Y. and Hirose, Y. (1968). *Kata of Kodokan judo*. Kobe: Koyano Bussan Kaisha Ltd.

Kotani, S. and Otaki, T. (1971). In Daigo, T. editor. (2008). *Kodokan Goshin-*

jutsu by [Saishin judo no kata]. Reprinted for the 2008 Kodokan Kata Kaki Koshukai (Kodokan Summer Kata Course). Tokyo: Kodokan Judo Institute.

Mori, O. (2008). *An introduction to Go no kata*. Tokyo: Private publication based on Kuhara, Y. (1976). *Judo Mizu Nagare*. Tokyo: Shudokan Kuhara Dojo. (in Japanese).

Murata, N. (2007). What is kata? The congratulatory address to the 1st Kodokan Judo Kata International Tournament. *Souvenir Program of the 1st Kodokan Judo Kata International Tournament 2007*, 26-27.

Murata, N. and Todo, Y. (2007). A study on evaluation of judo kata performance. *Bulletin of the Association for the Scientific Studies on Judo*, Kodokan. Report XI. (In Japanese, abstract in English.)

Murata, N. and Todo, Y. (2009). A study on evaluation of judo kata performance II Koshiki no Kata. *Bulletin of the Association for the Scientific Studies on Judo*, Kodokan. Report XII. (In Japanese, abstract in English).

Nogaki, P. (2009). Personal correspondence with Paul Nogaki on the ideals of kata.

Oda, J. (1929). *Judo taikan*. Tokyo: Shoshikan. (In Japanese).

Oltremari, A. (n.d.). Kata, sport e gare (Kata, sports and competition). Article online and available from freeBudo's website, URL:http://www.freebudo.com/articoli/judo%20tradizionale/articoli%20judo/1%20kata%20sport%20e%20gare/1%20kata%20sport%20e%20gare.htm (In Italian) (Retrieved, July 2010).

Otaki, T. and Draeger, D. (1983). *Judo formal techniques*. Tokyo: Charles E. Tuttle Company.

Pelletier, G. (n.d.). Kata. Article online and available from Guy Pelletier and André Andermatt's website, URL: http://pagesperso-orange.fr/pelletier.andermatt/5kata0.html (In French) (Retrieved, July 2010).

Sheedy, J. (2010). Judo kata competitions: A review of practice strategies for the Goshin Jitsu [*sic*]. Article online and available from the Judo Information website, URL: http://judoinfo.com/new/techniques/formsof-judo-kata/671-practice-strategies-for-goshin-jitsu (Retrieved, July 2010).

Sidney, J. (2003). *The warrior's path: Wisdom from contemporary martial arts masters*. Boston: Shambhala Publications.

Takamura, Y. (1986). Teaching and shu-ha-ri. Article online and available from the Takamura-ha Shindo Yoshin Kai website, URL: http://www.shinyokai.com/essays_teachingShuhari.htm (Retrieved, July 2010).

Ukichi, S. (n.d.) Matsumoto, T. and Davidson, P. translators. (n.d.) in Daigo, T. editor. (2008). *Eternal kendo*. Reprinted for the 2008 Kodokan Kata Kaki Koshukai (Kodokan Summer Kata Course). Tokyo: Kodokan Judo Institute.

chapter 6

A Taxonomy of Principles Used in Judo Throwing Techniques

by Linda Yiannakis, M.S.

All photographs courtesy of David J. Higgins.

Techniques and Variants

Judo offers many throwing techniques. Some are considered standard throws, while others are seen as variants of those throws. How can we identify exactly which throw we have seen, or even which throw we are practicing? While there are no hard and fast rules about defining variants, an examination of a technique's properties can help in the following ways:

1) to identify it
2) to address the critical properties for practicing it
3) to foster innovations
4) to help in teaching the technique to others

All of the techniques presented in the central throwing syllabus of judo, *Five Sets of Techniques* (Gokyo no waza, 1920) represent models of throwing. For a visual overview, points can be placed on a grid to represent techniques that form a systematic plan for teaching a complete repertoire of movements. Each throw is defined by what happens when it is executed: the general movement pattern or path, level of complexity, and associated actions such as reap, hook, sweep, etc.

Techniques, Principles, and Operative Ranges

Generally speaking, techniques are not principles. A principle is a law or property that operates consistently where it is applied. Techniques are identifiable sets of actions that are driven by principles. Principles have an optimal range of operation and are less effective or ineffective once outside that range. For example, to make best use of the principle of leverage in hip techniques, the thrower (*tori*) typically must drop his center of gravity below that of his partner or receiver of the action (*uke*). If he tries to apply leverage outside of this range of optimal operation he will have difficulty. Similarly, a successful foot sweep depends upon tori's sweeping action occurring at the moment uke transfers his weight onto or off of his foot. If uke's weight is fully on the target leg, the intended sweep is more likely to function as a kick. In other techniques, tori's and uke's relative positions will either help or hinder the best application of the principles for that particular technique, depending on the operative range of the principles involved.

CONSTRUCTION OF TECHNIQUE

We can better understand both the standard throwing forms and their variants by examining how the techniques are constructed. Each technique has a set of structural elements as well as internal operational principles or processes. We build techniques from combinations of structural elements and operational principles in a variety of configurations and directions of throwing. We can look at the structural and operational properties as discrete elements, but in actual application they overlap and integrate when techniques are executed.

Structural Elements:

1) the stance of both tori and uke
2) the physical orientation of tori to uke
3) the direction of the breaking of balance
4) the configuration of the fitting in and positioning portion of the throw (*tsukuri*)
5) the placement of limbs for various actions

We can call these features of placement, intended direction, and shape or contour of construction. As the actions of the throw progress, some of these elements of structure may shift. For example, the position or orientation of the arms in the pulling hand and the lifting hand may change as tori moves through the throw. We can see this in a technique such as the one-arm back-carry throw, where tori's lifting hand begins at the lapel but shifts across uke's body to a new position under his arm as tori moves into position. In the lifting-pulling hip throw, tori's stance and the relative positions of uke and tori shift as tori moves from a higher to lower position in front of uke. Looked at this way, structural elements are snapshots of critical features of tori's technique at particular moments during his performance of the throw.

Examples of Structural Elements

These photos illustrate various elements of structure, such as hand placement, leg placement, orientation of tori and uke, and higher or lower stance, at a particular point in the throw.

1) Major inner reaping throw. 2) Major outer reaping throw.
3) Lift-pull hip throw. 4) Major outer wheel.

Operational Principles:
1) centered action in body management and power generation
2) turning with conversion of energy
3) generating momentum (*hazumi*)
4) the actions of the pulling hand and the lifting hand
5) the active staging of the breaking of balance, positioning, and technique execution (*kuzushi*, *tsukuri*, and *kake*).

This category also includes:
6) the use of leverage, 7) sweeping, reaping, hooking, or other leg actions,
8) the sacrificing of the standing position, 9) winding or wrapping actions
10) "slipping by" actions, 11) other actions from tori's center

The structural elements of tori's orientation to uke and the placement of tori's hands, arms, or legs as he moves through a technique allow him to achieve the operations necessary for a particular throw. As an example, tori must achieve a certain orientation to uke and must place one leg outside of uke's leg in order to accomplish the reaping action in the major outer reaping throw. If he adopts a different orientation, i.e., turns his back to uke or places his leg between uke's legs, he will not be able to execute the major outer reaping throw. But he will be in position to move into a technique that has the structural and operational features for that orientation or leg placement, such as the inner thigh throw. The operational processes of the fitting-in stage of the throw are also often accompanied by changes in tori's arm placement, orientation to uke, or other structural characteristics.

Examples Using Operational Principles

1a–c: These illustrate tori's body control and turning in the big wheel throw.

2a–c: These show the use of momentum in the side wheel throw.

3a–c: These illustrate the principle of abandoning the standing position and using tori's dropping center to destabilize and throw uke.

Contextual Principles

Structural and operational principles may be supplemented by contextual principles. Contextual principles apply in situations or contexts of technique execution. This category includes principles:

1) initiative strategies (*sen*)
2) control of distance (*maai*)
3) creating momentum (*hazumi*)
4) yielding and redirecting (*ju*)
5) continuousness (*renzoku*)

Contextual principles operate in the interaction or synergy of movement between uke and tori. They may be applied as highly technical skills or as powerful, athletic movements. Some principles, such as the use of momentum, may operate both as a dynamic process internal to the throw (operational principle) and/or independently as a contextual principle. Judo players often work to create momentum when moving around with uke as a means of helping to establish the breaking of balance and allowing more efficient entry into techniques. Momentum can also be seen as an operational application within techniques such as the side wheel, the knee wheel, or the side drop, where internal momentum occurs as a result of tori's actions as he fits into the throw. Other contextual principles, such as continuousness (*renzoku*), aren't thought of as internal processes, but as operations that take place in the technique's environment. In the case of continuousness, two or more discrete techniques become seamlessly linked, but the principle itself is not part of the structural or operational features of the individual techniques that it brings together.

What tori does in the moments immediately before moving into a throw will directly affect how the operational principles of the technique come into play. Judo practitioners sometimes ask, "Which comes first, breaking balance or fitting into position?" While we summarize throwing principles as breaking balance, then fitting in, and finally execution, this is not a compartmentalized sequence of events that is engraved in stone. These three principles overlap and interact as a throw progresses. In either case, breaking balance and fitting in are complementary processes that culminate in the completion of the throw.

Without a doubt, execution is the final phase, but what about breaking balance and fitting in? Breaking balance may precede or follow the fitting-in stage, but in either case, it must be continuous after it has begun. Tori's actions in the context that gives rise to the technique determine which operational principles come into play next. If these contextual actions are dominated by a high degree of reliance on athleticism, power, speed, or superb timing, then the resulting processes of positioning may take precedence over the breaking of balance as an initiating element. That is to say, breaking balance may be a result of a dynamic fitting-in movement. As one example, tori may deal with uke by using strong gripping strategies both as a defensive maneuver and to prepare his own posture for a sudden drop under uke into a very low shoulder throw. Tori may drop into the throwing position with perfect timing and speed without necessarily destabilizing uke first. The breaking of balance occurs as tori moves rapidly through fitting in under uke and continues into the execution phase of the technique.

On the other hand, if elements such as the use of initiative strategies, control of distance, yielding and redirecting, action-reaction, or the seamless continuation of one technique into a second one are used to break the opponent's stance or to create an opening, then the breaking of balance may more likely precede positioning. Tori may attempt a knee wheel throw against uke's right knee, which uke evades by pulling or stepping back with his right foot. Tori, using the principle of continuousness, blends his movement with uke's retreating leg action and moves smoothly into a major outer reaping throw. Tori uses the energy and direction of uke's retreating action to stage the overbalancing of uke as tori continues into position for the major outer reaping throw.

Examples Using Contextual Principles
Using uke's energy or movement in combination techniques (*renzoku*) to unbalance the opponent (*kuzushi*) for a follow-up throw. These photographs (1a–d) show tori attempting a kneel wheel and uke retreating by pulling his attacked leg back. Tori blends his forward movement with uke's retreating movement and steps forward with his left foot into the major outer reaping throw.

These photographs (2a–d) show tori beginning a foot sweep on uke's left foot. As uke withdraws his left foot, tori continues sweeping his own right foot across to position it in front of uke's right foot. Tori continues to turn, and uses his rotation outward to unbalance uke and enters for a one-arm back carry throw.

The Standard Syllabus of Judo Throws and Katas

In judo the Kodokan's standard syllabus of throws is a primary resource for studying the structural and operational principles of techniques, and for understanding the relationships among the techniques. Prearranged forms such as *Nage-no-kata* (forms of throwing) fill out the study of techniques with examples of situations that require the application of a variety of contextual principles. For example, the first technique in Nage-no-kata is the floating drop. This technique provides lessons in responding to uke's advancing action with a synchronous retreating action. It also teaches tori to use control of distance as a means of staging overbalance. Tori's deliberately extended third step back increases the distance between himself and uke and breaks uke's posture forward for the throw's successful execution. The kata provides practice in executing techniques in dynamic interactions with uke that require the understanding of structural, operational, and contextual principles.

Moving out from the original central models in the Gokyo, we can also learn variations in techniques. These may involve changes in hand or leg placement or action, fitting-in actions, throwing direction, etc. Yet the throw may be still identified as the one of the same name in the Gokyo, or as a close relation. The variations may change some aspects of the outward appearance of the throw, but retain enough of its structural and operational features for a useful reference to the original. At times a throw that is essentially a variant of another has come to be regarded as a separate technique, rather than simply a variant. The one-arm back-carry throw was once considered a variant of the two-hand back-carry throw (Kano, 1986: 67). It is now placed as a separate technique in the newly accepted techniques of judo. Similarly, the minor outer hook was once regarded as a variant of the minor outer reap, but due to operational principles that differ, it stands on its own (Kano, 1986: 76).

One-arm back-carry throw (a–d).

Homogenization of Technique

At other times changes take place that result in a homogenization of technique so throws that are actually distinct become variants of each other. Although main elements may remain, some of the internal operational principles may get dropped out or changed. When this happens, the lines between techniques begin to blur. Throws that were placed in the Gokyo as separate techniques with distinct operations now coalesce into variants of each other. This happens largely in techniques with similar outward appearances.

As an example, we sometimes see the leg wheel and big wheel presented in modern judo as essentially the same throw. What differentiates them from each other in this way of thinking is primarily the leg placement: very high for the big wheel, and lower on the thigh for the leg wheel. In a case like this, the structural and operational principles that distinguish them from each other have been lost.

However, as actual distinguishing principles in the leg wheel, the leg acts to hold uke as tori turns out away from him, rotating uke over his outstretched leg. There is no sweeping or cutting action by the leg, and the leg placement can vary somewhat. In the big wheel, the situation is very different. The outstretched leg is quite active in the big wheel, uke must be extended farther forward by tori than in the leg wheel, and tori's leg makes a definite rotating action back toward uke.

In the leg wheel, uke is essentially rotated over a stationary barrier, while in the big wheel, the top part of his body is brought forward while the bottom half is pressed and actively rolled over through the action of tori's leg. These differing properties between the techniques require that more differences in action must take place beyond simply changing the position of the leg. When tori understands each technique's operational principles, he can address adopting any additional skills required for such differentiated techniques. This increased proficiency results in an expanded repertoire of movement skills. This type of understanding also provides instructors with additional resources for guiding and helping students to grasp the properties of techniques and to be better equipped to self-correct during their practice.

Similarly, we sometimes see the lifting hip throw taught as a version of the major hip throw with a belt hold. But *tsuri* refers to a particular action of lifting that doesn't occur in *ogoshi*. In order to achieve the tsuri action in the lifting hip throw, tori uses a type of hip action somewhat similar to that found in the floating hip throw, but with a fuller hip insertion somewhat closer to the major hip throw, as well as different corresponding upper-body actions.

As another example, the major outer wheel operates differently than the major outer reaping throw, and so is more than the major outer reaping throw done on both of uke's legs. The relative positions of uke and tori differ somewhat in the two techniques, as does the desired weight distribution on uke's legs and the actions needed by tori to achieve this for each technique. These differing structural and operational elements result in differing leg actions by tori against uke's leg(s) in the execution of the throw.

A variety of approaches to capturing different techniques occurs when uke and tori engage in free play or contest. The interplay of the many variables in movement between uke and tori provides opportunities for applying the contextual principles.

Kano organized the Gokyo as a guide to systematically teach the application of principles. He provided a curriculum of specific movement types and operations across increasing levels of complexity. When separate techniques become melded into variants without clear understanding of what has happened, some of that educational benefit is lost.

Showing Differences Between Techniques That Look Very Similar:
Leg wheel (*ashi guruma*) ↔ big wheel (*oguruma*)

Leg wheel throw. Tori's blocking leg is stationary and uke is rotated over it by tori's continued turning action.

Big wheel throw. Tori's outstretched leg actively rotates back into uke in this throw (2a–c).

Major outer reaping throw (*osoto gari*) ↔ major outer wheel (*osoto-guruma*)

Major outer reaping throw (l.). Tori drives uke back onto his right heel or outside of his right foot and then uses a reaping action to throw uke. **Major outer wheel** (r.). Tori drives uke back on both legs and rotates him over his outstretched leg.

Applicability to Contest

Someone who is interested in judo only as a competitive sport may not want as broad a curriculum as provided in the Gokyo. But it is still advantageous to understand the critical properties of the throws in individual competitive arsenals in order to make the techniques as powerful and as adaptable as possible in the high-speed, rapidly shifting demands of contest situations. An understanding of the original techniques' properties also allows for preservation of underlying processes and elements. These are important both in themselves and as a basis from which to consider innovation or to pass on to others.

Preservation and Change

Systems change over time in response to perceived needs or pressure from outside influences. One method of preservation and change in Japanese martial art is known as *shu ha ri* (Shimabukuro, 2008: 59-60). In this method, the preservation of the principles that define a system is built into whatever changes are made over the years. Any changes must conform to the defining principles of the system; otherwise, the very nature of the system becomes compromised. In the protective or imitative learning stage *shu* (守), the student strives to copy the teacher's actions as closely as possible, and to acquire a critical mass of the fundamentals on which the system is built. This stage lasts several years. In the change or divergence stage (*ha* 破), the student (now well into the black-belt level of the art) begins to move outside the boundaries of the carefully prescribed program of the ha stage. Nevertheless, his experimentation at this stage is still driven by close adherence to the principles that govern the system. He applies the fundamentals learned in the shu stage to more variations, or applies more individualistic interpretations of those fundamentals. In the final separation stage (*ri* 離), the student—now a high-ranking practitioner—has achieved a high level of understanding and skill within the system. In this stage, he moves out more freely into areas of innovation and transcends technical boundaries. He now has the knowledge to make changes to the system without corrupting its essential nature. In this way the art is both preserved and moved forward.

Judo has become subject to many changes over the years by high-ranking teachers at the Kodokan and elsewhere, as well as from the innovations that have arisen from competitors. However, coming from such diverse sources, modification in judo has not been entirely systematic, or necessarily in accord with the original principles of the system. This makes cataloging innovation much more difficult than if a process such as shu ha ri were in place today. For this reason, the framework of principles suggested in this paper may be helpful in allowing creative innovators to better articulate and share their contributions, as well as allowing them to see how their innovations fit into or change judo.

Summary

The essential principles underlying drive judo throwing techniques may be organized into *structural, operational,* and *contextual* categories. The elements and processes within these categories interact, overlap, and combine during the moving application of techniques.

The structural principles of technique may be thought of as those that answer questions that begin with "where" or "what," while the answer is a noun or an adverb: "What is my stance relative to uke?" "Where do I place my leg?" "Which is the optimal direction to off-balance an opponent?" Structural principles may be examined statically at any moment in time.

Operational principles of technique are those that mainly answer the question "How?" The answer involves a dynamic process or action. "How do I destabilize uke?" "How do I fit into position?" "How do I drop to the floor without pulling uke on top of me?"

Contextual principles answer the questions "when," "where," and "how," and are applied in the situation preceding or continuing into actual execution of the technique.

"When do I start my approach?" "Where do I enter for this technique?" "How do I make uke step so that I can apply the technique?" "How do I follow the first technique with the second?" These principles cannot occur in static isolation, but only during dynamic interactions.

We can practice techniques with structural and operational principles alone to highlight and clarify their operative processes. For example, all of judo's throwing techniques may be addressed individually in practice, if desired, with little or no resistance from uke. However, when studied in attack situations, free play, competitive "set-ups," contest, and routine practice (*kata*), they are supplemented with the contextual principles that allow them to be executed in an endless number of dynamic situations with a partner or opponent.

The framework presented here is offered as a tool and aid in clarifying the many overlapping, complex, and sometimes challenging actions that come together through best use of energy to result in the beautiful throws of Kano Jigoro's judo.

References

Daigo, T. (2005). *Kodokan judo throwing techniques*. Tokyo: Kodansha.
Kano, J. (1986). *Kodokan judo*. Tokyo: Kodansha International Ltd.
Shimabukuro, M., and Pellman, L. (2008). *Flashing steel: Mastering Eishin-Ryu swordsmanship, second edition*. Berkeley, CA: Blue Snake Books.

Acknowledgments

Many thanks to David J. Higgins for the photography and to Mark Fraser and Andrew Frye, who gave generously of their time and energy to serve as tori and uke in the illustrations for this chapter.

Judo Terminology

ashi-guruma	足車	leg wheel
Gokyo-no-waza	五教之技	five sets of techniques
hiza guruma	膝車	knee wheel
ippon seoi-nage	一本背負投	one-arm back-carry throw
kosoto gake	小外掛	minor outer hook
kosoto gari	小外刈	minor outer reap
kuzushi	崩し	breaking of balance
makikomi	巻込	winding or wrapping actions
morote seoi-nage	双手背負投	two-hand back-carry throw
Nage-no-kata	投の形	forms of throwing
nage-waza	投げ技	throwing techniques
ogoshi	大腰	major hip throw
oguruma	大車	big wheel
osoto-gari	大外刈	major outer reaping throw
osoto-guruma	大外車	major outer wheel
seiryoku zenyo	精力 善用	best use of energy
sukashi	透	"slipping by" actions
sutemi	捨身	sacrificing body position
tai sabaki	体捌き	body management
tenkan	転換	turning with conversion of energy
tsuri goshi	釣腰	lifting (belt) hip throw
tsuri komi goshi	釣込腰	lifting-pulling hip throw
uchi mata	内股	inner thigh throw
uki goshi	浮腰	floating hip throw
uki otoshi	浮落	floating drop
yoko guruma	横車	side wheel
yoko otoshi	横落	side drop

chapter 7

Rhythm, Patterns, and Timing in Martial Arts as Exemplified Through Judo

by Linda Yiannakis, M.S.

Introduction

We live in a world of patterns and rhythms. The tides roll, the seasons change, and our own internal rhythms ebb and flow. There are also patterns and rhythms that we create in our daily or weekly activities that we overlay on our lives and world.

Musashi, the great swordsman of seventeenth-century Japan, wrote about the importance to the martial artist of understanding timing and rhythm (*hyoshi*) in the Earth Scroll (*Chi no Maki*) from his book *Go Rin No Sho* (*The Book of Five Rings*):

> Rhythm is something that exists in everything, but the rhythms of martial arts in particular are difficult to master without practice. Rhythm is manifested in the world in such things as dance and music, pipes and strings. These are all harmonious rhythms. In the field of martial arts, there are rhythms and harmonies in archery, gunnery, and even horsemanship. In all arts and sciences, rhythm is not to be ignored. There is even rhythm in being empty.
> – Cleary, 1994: 30

How conscious are you of varying rhythms in your technique applications? Trying to barrel through every technique at exactly the same pace can result in frustration or failure. An awareness of rhythm in martial arts can help us fine-tune what we are trying to accomplish. The art of judo offers us a great many examples.

Judo practitioners should know that everything we do does not happen at the same speed or rhythm. Rhythm is not the same as speed. The Merriam-Webster dictionary defines speed as "swiftness or rate of performance or action: velocity." The definition of rhythm in reference to movement is given as "movement, fluctuation, or variation marked by the regular recurrence or natural flow of related elements." A movement's rhythm may therefore contain segments or cadences of varying speeds, and may be perceived as a pattern. While speed or lack of speed of application is something we can see easily in judo, rhythms can be subtler and less apparent unless we are looking for them.

Contextual Processes

One way to think about achieving an entry to a throw is to add a consideration of rhythms to the "when" and "how" of our approach to the receiver of the action (*uke*). What are the elements of rhythm that bring the thrower (*tori*) right to uke's doorstep, so to speak? These involve the movements that allow tori to be in position to move into the fitting-in phase (*tsukuri*) of the technique. These actions occur in the context immediately preceding tori's initiation of his entry, and contribute to his being in the right place at the right time. At this point in tori's impending attack we can see patterns emerge in the use of a variety of strategies and principles, such as gripping strategies, stepping patterns, body management (*tai-sabaki*), the creation of momentum, and others.

Sidebar — Uke and Tori: Uke and tori are designations for roles taken by two judo players in interactions with each other. Uke receives the action tori makes. Tori may be executing a throw, or just fitting in for one—or he may be applying a choke, armbar, pin, or other action against uke. Uke may be cooperative and compliant, or he may resist tori's actions in a variety of ways, but the relationship is the same. Although the dynamics of the interaction change in different situations, uke is ultimately the receiver of an action that tori completes.

Stepping Pattern

When you use a normal walk (*ayumi ashi*), a following step (*tsugi ashi*), or another type of movement, you can establish directional patterns. The basic, common patterns are (1) advancing straight forward, (2) retreating straight backward, (3) moving laterally to the left or the right, (4) moving forward to the left or right corner, (5) moving backward to the left or right corner, and (6) circling. Each of these patterns may be performed at a variety of speeds or combined with another. Of course, these directions are only selected, representative points from 360 degrees of possibility of movement, but they allow you to structure your practice in the major directions.

Speed

Every encounter is characterized by a particular speed or tempo, which may vary throughout the interaction. One partner may seek to control the tempo while the other partner either follows or attempts to impose his own pace. Tempo can vary from nonstop, rapid motion to slow, almost static, cautious stepping.

Stride Length

The length of your stride, or the space between one step and the next, varies from judoka to judoka, from technique to technique, and sometimes between defensive and offensive movement.

Rhythms in Pattern Matching

How do we actually use the understanding of rhythms to improve our positioning for an entry in free play or contest? It is easy to become familiar with various rhythms in gross movements by starting with exercises that center on matching patterns with your partner using the characteristics identified above.

Mirroring

A simple exercise is to work with a cooperative partner and have one person follow the other's movements by mirroring them. The two take grips, and the leader begins the exercise by moving in a relaxed manner, in natural posture (*shizentai*), in any direction he chooses. The follower's job is to mirror his partner's relaxed posture and movements. Without resistance, this exercise allows both participants to concentrate on fluid, centered action, and to be aware of their partner's movements and changes in direction.

The mirroring exercise can be modified in many ways. One way to change it is to require the follower to mirror the leader, but to follow reluctantly. The follower gives some resistance, but still mirrors the leader's pattern. The leader then has to focus on maintaining fluid movement and making his follower move by use of the leader's own centered action, and not by muscling or yanking to make his partner follow.

Resistance by the follower can be ramped up in stages to full-fledged resistance in the defensive posture called *jigotai*, if desired. The leader's objective remains the same: to move his partner using centered action, and not with a reliance on upper-body strength. By changing the follower's role, both participants can experience discerning the other's movement patterns under varying conditions of cooperation and resistance.

Stepping Pattern in Mirroring

When using the mirroring exercise, the leader can focus on particular patterns of movement at any level of resistance by the follower. The six basic directional patterns are discussed above. The leader can choose one, two, or all six patterns to move through as he leads his partner, who must perceive each movement and follow seamlessly. These exercises can also be expanded by requiring the leader to change directions and to make entries into throws with adequate overbalancing in all of the directions of movement. As the agreed-upon resistance by the follower increases, the leader will need to continue to use centered action to achieve the overbalance. If he finds that he is beginning to rely on too much muscle power to break his partner's posture, he should drop back to a step with less resistance by the follower and work more at that level.

Speed in Mirroring

The leader chooses movement directions and the level of resistance from the follower. He also chooses the speed at which he will move through his patterns or into his entries. The follower must match the speed. The leader may vary the tempo throughout the movement exercise, and his partner must match this and the changes in direction of movement, as well as maintain the desired level of cooperation or resistance.

Stride Length in Mirroring

Finally, the leader also establishes a particular stride length as he leads his partner through the mirroring exercise. As with the first two elements described above, the leader may change this feature at will during the exercise. The follower must match stride length as well as direction and speed of movement throughout the exercise.

Varying the Elements of Rhythm and Pattern

By varying the main factors of direction or stepping pattern, speed, and stride length, the leader gains experience in moving efficiently in a variety of ways. He also must achieve overbalance of his partner and be able to move into position for a throw under a variety of conditions. In addition, he becomes more aware of commonly occurring patterns involving all of these elements. As the leader establishes patterns or rhythms and then continually changes them throughout the interaction, the follower's awareness of these patterns, rhythms, and changes to them by his partner is also enhanced through this structured exercise.

The exercise may be further expanded by the following:
1) requiring work on both left- and right-side techniques,
2) specifying different grips,
3) continually shifting posture from natural to defensive and back,
4) requiring partners to work in same stance or opposite stance (*kenka yotsu*),
5) limiting the types of throws the leader may attempt (i.e., just hip techniques; just sweeps, etc.),
6) focusing on awareness of the follower's weight transfers onto and off of his feet as he moves,
7) requiring the follower to block, evade, or counter each time the leader makes an entry, or

8) requiring the leader to focus on continuous combination attacks (*renzoku waza*), and

9) any other feature you want to build into the exercise.

Disruption of Rhythm

When engaged in free play (*randori*) or in contest, we don't want to get caught in the predictability of an established pattern or rhythm. Further, if we match our partner's pattern for more than a step or two at a time, it can be difficult to achieve overbalance or begin an entry for a throw because he will see the pattern match and be ready to block or counter. But establishing, however briefly, any of the movement patterns mentioned above in order to disrupt them provides the thrower (*tori*) with an opportunity to move into his throw.

Yagyu Munenori, head of the Yagyu Shinkage-ryu in the seventeenth century, wrote, "Deliver the kind of strokes that do not harmonize with the opponent's strokes" (Tabata, 2003: 6). Although he was referring to swordwork, the same principle applies to other types of movement.

Tori may set up a particular stepping pattern that uke follows or responds to, even if only for a couple of steps. For example, tori may initiate a series of small, advancing steps (or even one advancing step). Uke may then retreat in response. As soon as tori perceives that uke has fallen into the pattern, he disrupts the rhythm by stepping sideways or diagonally, or by changing his speed or stride length. This sudden change, controlled by tori, gives him a small opportunity to attack outside of the brief rhythm of the pattern, where uke is not expecting him to move.

Setting and Disrupting a Stepping Pattern

Mark and Andrew begin in the left natural posture (*hidari shizentai*) (A1). Mark steps forward with his right foot. Andrew mirrors this by stepping back with his left foot (A2). Mark then disrupts this brief pattern by stepping out to the side with his left foot, drawing Andrew off balance as he does so (A3). Uke: Andrew Frye; Tori: Mark Fraser

As an example, tori initiates the advancing pattern with his right foot in preparation for moving into a major outer reaping throw (*osoto-gari*) to uke's rear. If uke retreats with his left leg, tori can continue to move forward with uke's backward movement. As tori then begins to advance with his left foot, uke retreats with his right. But here tori allows his left leg to lag behind for just a brief moment. This allows uke time to complete his withdrawing movement with his right leg and to transfer his weight to it, which is what tori wants for this throw. At the moment uke commits his weight to his right leg, tori changes his speed and stride length to bring his left foot forward and then achieve placement of his reaping (right) leg against uke's now-weighted right leg. Tori has implemented a rhythm of slowing down and then suddenly speeding up. This control of tempo in the approach to the throw provides tori an opportunity to attack uke's leg before he has a chance to move it farther back and out of reach. It gives tori the opportunity for a more efficient attack by reducing the problem of having to catch up to uke's retreating leg before uke transfers the weight off of it as he continues moving backward.

Timing the Entry for the Major Outer Reaping Throw (Osoto-gari)
Mark steps forward with his right foot, and Andrew responds by stepping back with his left foot (B1). Mark then presses forward and begins to move his left foot forward, but allows it to lag slightly behind (B2). Andrew, expecting Mark to take a full step forward with his left as he had with his right, steps back with his right (B3). As soon as Andrew's weight is committed to his right leg, Mark moves in quickly for a major outer reaping throw (B4).
Uke: Andrew Frye; Tori: Mark Fraser

Uke's Rhythm

Just as important as the rhythms you initiate and control as tori are the rhythms that uke puts in place. Uke will also establish various stepping patterns, speeds, and stride lengths. You need to be aware of exactly what uke is doing. By honing your awareness and perception of his actions, you can use the same methods of disruption that you use when you establish the pattern, by altering any of the elements of direction, speed, or stride length (or a combination of these).

For example, let's say uke has begun to retreat. He can be using any type of stepping movement, taking small, cautious steps or longer, more definitive steps backward. As tori, you can follow him in this pattern and try to achieve a throw to uke's rear. Or, you can suddenly disrupt the pattern and timing with a rapid "jumping in" entry to the front, where you allow his legs to continue to retreat but keep his upper body drawn forward as you enter for a sweeping loin throw (*harai goshi*), a back carry throw (*seoi-nage*), or other forward throw. Similarly, you can disrupt his pattern by stepping sideways or to the corner, or by imposing your own rhythm by speeding up or slowing down.

Once the entry has been achieved, there are further rhythms to consider: those that occur as part of completing the positioning and execution of the throw. At that point we are considering the operational principles, or the dynamic processes, of the technique itself.

Operational Processes and Internal Rhythms

It is clear to most judoka that different techniques have different "feels" to them. Those differences arise partly from the various actions that tori makes with his torso, arms, and legs as he fits in and disturbs uke's balance, but also from the differences in timing that result from these varied actions. Thus different techniques can be seen to have their own unique rhythms. For example, the thrower's timing for the side separation throw (*yoko wakare*) can seem abrupt when compared to the rhythm of coming around his partner to enter for the side wheel throw (*yoko guruma*). By the same token, the timing for the advanced foot sweep (*de ashi barai*) is very different from the timing for a larger technique, such as the major hip throw (*ogoshi*) or the large wheel throw (*oguruma*).

My sensei's sensei, Taizo Sone, used to tell him, "*Waza wa hito nari.*" The sense of this phrase is that the technique takes on a life of its own. You need time for all of these movements and forces to come together and play out in their unique rhythmic patterns. You must consider the interaction of tori, uke, and the dynamics of the technique itself.

The time we are speaking of is fractions of a second. This is easy to see in foot sweeps, where sweeping slightly too soon or too late will result in a failed technique. A mistimed, early sweep in the following or double foot sweep (*okuri ashi barai*) or in the lifting-drawing foot sweep (*harai tsurikomi ashi*) provides lessons in the understanding of the need for a little patience in the execution of certain techniques.

As another example, it is useful to compare the control of rhythm in the major outer reaping throw (*osoto-gari*) with the minor outer hooking throw (*ko soto gake*). Both of these techniques throw uke to the rear. In the major outer reaping throw, tori's inside leg is used to create a large reaping motion against uke's near leg. In the minor outer hooking throw, tori's outside leg comes across to uke's near leg in a hooking motion.

For the minor outer hook, tori advances with his right foot and uke retreats with his left foot, as in the example of the major outer reaping throw described previously. Now tori has set up the suggestion of a pattern of movement. Tori next inclines his upper body slightly and begins to bring his left leg forward as if to advance with his left. Instead, as uke withdraws his right leg, tori lets his left foot lag behind while he allows his left hand to follow uke's movement backward. As uke steps down onto his withdrawn right foot, tori changes rhythm by very quickly moving his left foot ahead so it is outside of uke's right. Just as quickly, he skips his right foot forward to take the place of his left, which then presses against the outside/back of uke's right foot and clips it out from under him in a hooking movement as tori continues to drive forward with his center through the technique.

While this "lagging" method utilizes rhythm in the same manner as in the major outer reaping throw, the rhythms in each of the two techniques feel quite different due to the dynamics of leg movement and placement for tori's inside leg or his outside leg, as well as differences in the upper-body movements for each throw.

Perceiving the Pattern Change in Combination Attacks

Judoka often use techniques in combinations. Combinations may be done as discrete, sequential techniques, often in an action-reaction dynamic. This type of combination is known as *renraku waza*, in which the techniques are connected in sequence. Combinations may also be done as *renzoku waza*, in which the second technique flows continuously from the action of the first technique. Both types of combinations require that tori initiate an approach or entry to a throw. In effect, a throw is a pattern of specific movement involving breaking of posture (*kuzushi*), fitting in (*tsukuri*), and, if successful, execution (*kake*). However, if uke detects the initiation of the pattern in time, he will move to disrupt it by evading, blocking, or countering with a technique of his own. When tori initiates a technique, he must be aware of any shifts in movement that uke makes so that tori can follow uke's shift with a second technique—a combination—based on what uke has done to disrupt tori's original pattern or throw. Essentially, the thrower begins a pattern, uke disrupts it, and the thrower follows uke's disruption with a second technique. Successful combination throwing depends upon tori's ability to perceive pattern changes made by uke and to respond to them with appropriate follow-up movements.

Changing the Rhythm for the Minor Outer Hook (Ko Soto Gake)

Andrew steps forward with his right foot and Mark retreats with his left foot in response (C1). Andrew then begins to bring his left leg forward as if to advance with his left but lets his left foot lag behind while Mark steps back with his right foot (C2). Andrew allows his left hand to follow Mark's movement backward (C3). As Mark steps down onto his withdrawn right foot, Andrew changes rhythm by quickly moving his left foot forward outside of Mark's right (C4). Just as quickly, he skips his right foot forward to replace his left, and then presses his left foot against the outside/back of Mark's right foot and clips it out from under him in a hooking movement as he drives through the technique (C5).

Uke: Mark Fraser; Tori: Andrew Frye.

Other Applications of Rhythm: Repetitive Practice

A common exercise in judo is repetitive fitting practice, or *uchi-komi*. There are many ways to perform this exercise, but we will use a basic, common method as the example here. In this method of repeated practice, uke stands in whatever posture the thrower, tori, designates—usually basic natural posture, or right or left natural posture, but it can also be defensive posture. The thrower selects one technique at a time for his repetitive practice exercise. He enters for the throw, bringing uke into an overbalanced position, but does not complete the throw beyond that point of overbalance. The thrower then reverses his movement and returns to his starting position. Typically, an uchi-komi exercise like this will be repeated a set number of times in rapid succession. It is sometimes extended to include an actual throw at the end of the repetitions, when tori will complete the technique and execute the throw on the final entry. For example, tori may perform nine rapid entries with overbalance for the sweeping hip throw, and on the tenth trial complete the technique, taking uke over and to the ground. Then tori will begin another round of repeated practice with the same throw or with a different one.

For uchi-komi to be beneficial, each of tori's entries must contain all of the necessary elements for a successful completion of the throw. This means that if tori is doing rounds of ten—nine entries plus one throw—each entry must look and feel and operate like the final one when tori actually throws uke. If the entries preceding the final throw in each set are different from the final product, the exercise has not contributed to tori's practice of actually throwing. The final throw should be a smooth continuation of the entry and off balancing that tori has achieved in each of his first nine entries in that set of repeated practice.

One of the benefits of this type of practice is the use of rhythm as an organizing device in the construction of throws. As tori moves smoothly in and out through his ten entries and into his final throw, he establishes an overall rhythm that helps him bring together the various elements of off balancing, fitting in, and correct body and limb orientation to uke for optimal efficiency in each particular throw. When tori switches to a different throw, or type of throw (e.g., from a hip throw to a foot sweep), he finds that the overall rhythm changes because the internal elements and operational processes of the two throws are different from each other. The rhythmic pattern that tori creates for each technique in repeated practice exercises helps him to coordinate all of the necessary forces at the right time for smooth and efficient throwing and to develop a feel for each type of technique.

The organizing concept of rhythm in uchi-komi is also found in repetitive throwing practice, or *nagekomi*. Nagekomi also involves awareness of appropriate rhythms as tori performs repeated throws, whether standing still or moving. When moving, tori must find the best moment of opportunity to begin his throw, and must wrap this together with all of the critical elements that come into play as part of the throw itself.

Repetitive Practice
Here Mark sets up a rhythm that organizes his movements during repetitive practice (*uchi-komi*). Uke: Andrew Frye; Tori: Mark Fraser

Falling or Receiving (Ukemi)

Another area where we can see the use of rhythm is in the practice of falling ways. Ukemi practice can be structured to make use of rhythm as an organizing force in various exercises. The standard method for practicing falling as part of or after a warm-up involves performing back, side, and front falls and rolls from varied distances from the floor. Key points include attention to breathing, controlling the head and body in space, and managing the impact properly. But in addition to these important elements, falling practice can facilitate body control through attention to the rhythm of the movements.

Self-Defense Techniques (Goshin Waza)

Striking techniques in judo (*atemi waza*) are jujutsu strikes and were developed to be used as an end in themselves and as a means of breaking posture (*kuzushi*) to allow entry into throwing, joint locking, or strangling techniques. Overall rhythms in an exchange with an opponent will vary according to type of offense or defense involved, directionality, and intensity of the opponent's movement, as well as environmental factors such as terrain, obstacles, walls, additional attackers, involvement of weapons, and tori's ultimate intentions for the outcome of the encounter (to escape, to immobilize the assailant, or to cause injury to the assailant). The timing and rhythm of judo atemi waza and other self-defense techniques fit into this larger whole of closing distance while moving into the opponent to finish the encounter.

Other Examples of Larger Rhythms: Types of Initiatives

Each of the major types of combat initiatives—direct (*sen*), following or countering (*gonosen*), or leading (*sen sen no sen*)—involves its own timing. The rhythm of gonosen, for example, involves a period of waiting—a very short period—that does not occur in the same way in a direct initiative attack. The "go" in gonosen refers to something "behind" or "after"—your attack must follow behind or after another attack. The rhythm of initiation in gonosen is governed by tori's perceiving uke's attack and allowing it to proceed to a certain point. At that time tori collects the energy that uke has given him and counters with his own technique, utilizing the motion and energy provided by uke. The difference may at times be subtle between a lightning-fast counter and a rapid direct attack, but ignoring these subtle differences between sen and gonosen may result in tori's rushing the counter. A counter that is attempted too early in uke's attack may end with uke's blocking or evading the counter, and tori's failure. Each of the three main initiative types is characterized by timing appropriate to its approach and implementation of technique.

Countering the Inner Thigh Throw (uchi-mata) with a Hip Throw

Mark attempts a right-side inner thigh throw (uchi-mata) (E1). Andrew waits for the appropriate moment (E2), evades Mark's leg (E3), takes Mark's energy (E4), and moves into a left-side hip throw to counter (use of gonosen) (E5). Uke: Mark Fraser; Tori: Andrew Frye

Countering the Major Outer Reaping Throw (osoto-gari) with the Floating Drop (ukiotoshi)

Andrew approaches Mark for a major outer reaping throw (osoto-gari) (F1). As Andrew commits himself to reaping his leg through (F2), Mark evades the reap by stepping back and dropping (F3), countering Andrew's major outer reaping throw with a floating drop (ukiotoshi) (F4-5). Uke: Andrew Frye; Tori: Mark Fraser

Kata

The various forms (*kata*) of judo provide opportunities to observe, study, and work within prescribed rhythms for the specific purposes of each kata. Draeger (1983: 133) calls attention to the differences in the overall rhythms of the Forms of Throwing (*Nage no Kata*) and the Forms of Grappling (*Katame-no-Kata*):

> Unlike *Nage no Kata*, this kata [*Katame-no-kata*] is a mixture of paces or tempos, easy to recognize, but quite difficult to achieve except for the most experienced judoists. The burden of keeping the proper rhythm rests with Tori, who frequently must move in and out on both the lateral and longitudinal axes as well as between them to apply his techniques .... Hesitations and mistakes in positioning by either partner make for bad timing and easily shatter the rhythm of this kata. As an alternation of slow, smoothly executed preliminary movements and faster, more actively executed techniques, this kata lacks the metronomic rhythm of the Nage no Kata.

Within Nage no Kata itself, a use of similar rhythm was noted by Leggett in both the opening and closing techniques as they were done in earlier days:

> Ukiotoshi is the simplest of throws in principle—rhythm is imposed on uke, and then the very long step breaks the rhythm and uke cannot recover psychologically in time to adapt. In Ukiwaza at the end, tori reverts to the same principle, including the long step.
> – Leggett, 1982: 69

Similarly, practice of the Forms of Gentleness (*Ju no Kata*) involves a study of moments of opportunity for evading and countering continuing attacks. A harmonious rhythm is built from perceiving and reacting to actions, countering actions, and countering the countering actions. "One must manage timing by blending with the partner, demonstrating the principle of Ju in reciprocal Taisabaki.... The pair must make an effort to move accurately and smoothly by the practice of correct timing" (Fukuda, 2004: 6).

Other katas of Kodokan judo also include studies of rhythm and timing related to the principles expressed in those forms.

Summary

Timing, patterns, and rhythm in martial arts play an important role, one that is too often overlooked. Understanding, perceiving, and directing the many rhythms involved before and during an exchange can give you an added edge in an encounter. Although each is brief in nature, the successive rise and fall of rhythms during a confrontation can constitute significant elements of the interaction. Learning to perceive and act on these rhythms is an important part of training.

As Musashi advises:

> The rhythms of the martial arts are varied. First know the right rhythms and understand the wrong rhythms, and discern the appropriate rhythms from among great and small and slow and fast rhythms. Know the rhythms of spatial relations, and know the rhythms of reversal. These matters are specialties of martial science. Unless you understand these rhythms of reversal, your martial artistry will not be reliable.
>
> The way to win in a battle according to military science is to know the rhythms of the specific opponents, and use rhythms that your opponents do not expect, producing formless rhythms from rhythms of wisdom. . . . In individual martial arts it also happens that an adversary will get out of rhythm in combat and start to fall apart. If you let such a chance get by you, the adversary will recover and thwart you. It is essential to follow up firmly on any loss of poise on the part of an opponent, to prevent him from recovering.
>
> – Cleary, 1994: 31; 91-92

Bibliography

Aida H. and Harrison, E.J., trans. (1956). *Kodokan judo*. London: W. Foulsham.
Cleary, T., trans. (1994). *The book of five rings*. Boston: Shambhala.
Fukuda, K. (2004). *Ju-no-kata: A Kodokan textbook*. Berkeley: North Atlantic.
Koizumi, G. (1960). *My study of judo*. New York: Cornerstone Library.
Ishikawa, T., and Draeger, D. (1999). *Judo training methods*. Boston: Tuttle.
Leggett, T.P., and Kano, J. (1982). *Kata judo*. London: W. Foulsham and Co.
Leggett, T.P. and Watanabe, K. (1994). *Championship judo*. London: Ippon Books.
Otaki, T. and Draeger, D. (1983). *Judo formal techniques*. Vermont: Tuttle.
Tabata, K. (2003). *Secret tactics: Lessons from the great masters of martial arts*. Boston: Tuttle Publishing.
Tokitsu, K. (2005). *Miyamoto Musashi: His life and writings*. Boston: Weatherhill.
Wilson, W.S., trans. (2002). *The book of five rings: Miyamoto Musashi*. Tokyo: Kodansha International Ltd.

chapter 8

Kodokan Judo's Self-Defense System: Kodokan Goshin-jutsu

by Llyr C. Jones, Ph.D., Martin P. Savage, B.Ed.
and W. Lance Gatling, M.A., M.P.S.

Introduction

Kodokan[1] *Judo* (judo) [the flexible way] developed by Jigoro Kano *shihan* [head teacher[2]] (1860-1938) is an all-round cooperative education, teaching system (pedagogy) and philosophy—based *inter alia* on conservative Confucianism values, *koryu*[3] [traditional (or old) school] *jujutsu* [flexible art, "the old samurai art of fighting without weapons" (Lindsay and Kano, 1889)] and European liberal educational philosophy (Stevens, 2013: 43). In particular, judo emphasizes the holistic educational value of training in attack and defense, so that it can be a "path", or way of life, that all people can participate in and benefit from.

Judo's *Kodokan Goshin-jutsu* [literally *Kodokan Self Defense Techniques*] is an exercise developed in the early 1950s by that era's greatest Kodokan teachers, including Hideichi Nagaoka, Kyuzo Mifune, Kaichiro Samura, Shozo Nakano, Tamio Kurihara, Sumiyuki Kotani, Tadao Otaki, Kenji Tomiki, and others. Today, Kodokan Goshin-jutsu is included in the list of *kata* [forms] officially recognized by the Kodokan.

Purpose, Scope and Structure of this Chapter

Finding information about the technical contents and mechanics of Kodokan Goshin-jutsu is not difficult. Having existed for just sixty years, it is the youngest of all the Kodokan kata, and is well documented by some of the main people involved in its development. Moreover, since Kodokan Goshin-jutsu dates from after Kano's death, there are no original writings by the Shihan, nor any rare historic books on the exercise to be found. However, the texts that go beyond describing Kodokan Goshin-jutsu's mechanical movements (be they in Japanese, English or another Western language) are either out of print or rare, and this makes accessing detailed information on its historical background, theoretical foundations and fundamental principles more challenging.

To address this challenge the present chapter, published to coincide with the sixty-year anniversary of the establishment of Kodokan Goshin-jutsu, provides an accessible and detailed English language study into the exercise. In doing so it contributes to furthering judo knowledge. However, presenting full details on how to perform the complete Kodokan Goshin-jutsu is out of scope, and for this, the reader is directed to the various learning resources referenced herein. In terms of organization, this chapter follows a structure analogous to that found in other work on kata by De Crée and Jones (2009; 2011) and De Crée (2015).

THE POSITION OF KODOKAN GOSHIN-JUTSU IN THE KODOKAN KATA

Kata in Judo

Kata are "formal movement pattern exercises containing idealized model movements illustrating specific combative principles" (Kawamura and Daigo, 2000: 86)—which together with *randori* [free practice], *kogi* [lectures] and *mondo* [dialogue] comprise the four critical pillars of Kodokan judo education (De Crée and Jones, 2009; 2011; De Crée, 2015).

Writing (in Japanese) in the early Kodokan journal, "*Sakko*" ["*Awakening*"], Kano explained how judo's kata were formulated in response to the fact that the number of students at the Kodokan was growing, and that he himself could not directly teach each one individually:

> In those [early] days I taught kata personally, to each student, but gradually their numbers increased. To give all students individual instruction became a very time-consuming process… It was shortly thereafter that I realised that new judo kata were needed.
> – Kano, n.d. cited in Watson, 2008

In this context, kata are merely short, predetermined attack and defense sequences that are both a teaching tool, and a training drill. However, in judo, what are most often thought of as kata are the formally recorded sets of choreographed techniques synthesized to illustrate specific principles. Cornish (2004) calls these exercises the "listed kata".

The Listed Kata

In his opening lecture to the 2008 Kodokan Summer Kata Course, Toshiro Daigo[4] gave a brief overview, with some history, of nine "official" listed kata currently recognized by the Kodokan—see Table 1.

Table 1
Nine "Listed Kata" of Kodokan Judo and Their
Contribution to Learning *Ju-no-ri* [principle of flexibility]

Kata	Intellectual &/or Moral	Physical Conditioning	Attack & Defense	Aesthetic
Nage-no-kata [forms of throwing]	●	▲	●	▲
Katame-no-kata [forms of grappling / holding]	●	▲	●	▲
Kime-no-kata [forms of decisive techniques]	▲		●	
Ju-no-kata [forms of gentleness & flexibility]		●	▲	▲
Kodokan Goshin-Jutsu [Kodokan self-defense]	●		●	
Itsutsu-no-kata [five forms]	●			●
Koshiki-no-kata [ancient forms]	●		▲	●
Go-no-kata [forms of (proper use of) force]		●		
Sei-ryoku-zen'yo Kokumin-Taiiku [forms of maximum efficiency national physical education]		●	▲	

Key: ● Significant ▲ Less Significant

Daigo's lecture notes (Daigo, 2008) included, inter alia, translated extracts from Kotani and Otaki's 1971 book *Saishin Judo-no-Kata Zen* [*The Latest Judo Kata Complete*] (Kotani and Otaki, 1971) and also from *Kodokan Judo-no-Kata* [*The Kata of Kodokan Judo*] published by the Kodokan in 1964 (Showa 39). Moreover, the lecture subsequently formed the basis of Daigo's comprehensive, multi-part article on kata—"Kodokan Judo Kata ni Tsuite" ["About the Kata of Kodokan Judo"], which was serialized in seven parts in the

Kodokan's periodical *Judo* from October 2008 to April 2009 (Daigo, 2008-2009).

The nine kata each contain various spheres of principles that help teach the *judoka* [a person who practices judo] the overall meaning of *ju-no-ri* [principle of flexibility]—where one avoids directly opposing an opponent's force and power, in favor of using it to one's own advantage (Kawamura and Daigo, 2000: 83).

While not a means of formally grouping[5] the various kata per se, Table 1 shows how these principles come to the fore in each kata (Osamu Mouri, personal communication, 13 September 2015).

In counting nine Kodokan kata, Daigo omits the female self-defense kata, *Joshi Goshin-ho*, which is an officially sanctioned, but uncommon Kodokan kata[6] (De Crée and Jones, 2011). Additionally, such counting ignores both *Kime Shiki* [forms of decision] and *Ju Shiki* [forms of gentleness]—two kata that were considered as distinct in the past, but today are regarded as being part of Sei-ryoku-zen'yo Kokumin-Taiiku.

Underlying Principles

Towards the end of his life Jigoro Kano (at the age of 75) wrote an important short article on general principles in judo—"The True Significance of Judo and the Purpose of Training" (Kano, 1934 in Imperial Japan Oratory Society, 1934). In the article Kano explained that all applications in judo were created from the fundamental principle of *seiryoku zen'yo* [best use of energy]. Originally in Japanese:

> I taught the principles [of judo], not the application of the principles...
> If something goes wrong with the application [technique], be it technical or mental, then return to the basic principles and test how closely they are reflected in the application.
>
> ...if any of the techniques do not conform to the principles, then they are not my teachings, and a mistake has been made in the application of the principle...
>
> – Ibid.

This approach goes directly to the very heart of judo, and indicates, *inter alia*, that kata is not an application, or mere mechanical movements, but rather, is a direct expression of judo's *riai*[7] [underlying principles]. For example, the 15 techniques in Nage-no-kata were deemed sufficient to learn the principles of the entire *Gokyo no waza* [five sets of techniques]—the standard syllabus of judo throwing techniques for randori (O. Mouri, personal communication, 25 January 2007).

Moreover, the principles are timeless and unbounded, and so, for example, Nage-no-kata is equally relevant for learning the Gokyo's subsequent evolutions and additions, such as the *Shinmeisho-no-waza* [newly accepted techniques]. Principles are also subliminal, and in regular practice today, almost every judoka is actually applying principles that can be found, for example, in Koshiki-no-kata, whether or not they have any knowledge of that particular form, or awareness that they are doing so (Ibid.).

Is Kodokan Goshin-jutsu a kata or not, and why?

Kodokan Goshin-jutsu is not called *Kodokan-Goshin-jutsu-no-kata* [forms of Kodokan self-defense], though this inaccurate name quite often features in some of the less informed material on the exercise. Given the intentional omission of "*-no-kata*" from the name, it is valid to pose the question "Is Kodokan Goshin-jutsu a kata or not, and why?" To address this issue, this study will use reliable and pertinent material from both primary and secondary sources.

From one standpoint, the compact, but comprehensive, *Kodokan New Japanese-English Dictionary of Judo* by Kawamura and Daigo (2000) indicates that Kodokan Goshin-jutsu is a kata. This perspective of course is consistent with its present-day treatment by the Kodokan:

> Kodokan Goshinjutsu (Kodokan Self-Defense Forms): A set of Kodokan Judo formal exercises (kata) designed to teach ways and means of self-defense using throwing, grappling and striking techniques, formally devised in 1956 to meet modern needs.
> – Ibid.: 92

However, the literature also contains alternative standpoints, also from serious sources. For example, Steven Cunningham[8] presently USJA[9] 6th dan in an interview with Linda Yiannakis, discusses the content and development of several judo kata, including Kodokan Goshin-jutsu. The interview was serialized as a two-part article in *American Judo*—the journal of the USJA. Therein, Yiannakis (2002: 19-21; 2003, 20-24) reports Cunningham's observations:

> Also in the Kodokan syllabus is the Kodokan Goshin-jutsu. Notice that it isn't called Goshin-jutsu no Kata. This is because the Goshin-jutsu is thought to be a plan of study of self-defense techniques (*goshin waza*), as opposed to being formally a kata, although it's often demonstrated that way.
> – Yiannakis, 2002: 20

Cunningham is therefore explaining that it was not intended for Kodokan Goshin-jutsu to be a kata, in the proper sense of "kata", but rather a collection of techniques grouped together to represent defenses against several kinds of attack.

Arguably, the most authoritative answer to the original question comes from Daigo. In a personal exchange, first formally reported in De Crée and Jones (2011), Daigo expressed a revised position to the one he had implied earlier (Kawamura and Daigo, 2000; Daigo, 2008-09):

> There are no kata after the death of Kano Jigoro. Sei-ryoku zenyo kokumin taiiku was never meant to be a kata (solely) for judoka but for general physical education (for the general public). Joshi goshinho is more an application than a set of principles, thus consequently intended to be more practical, which is understandable, particularly if we consider the social environment in which it was made by Nango.[10] For the same reason, Kodokan Goshin-jutsu is not given a suffix of '-kata'.
>
> – De Crée and Jones, 2011

Daigo's statement is unambiguous—Kodokan Goshin-jutsu is not a kata in the strictest of formal senses, even though today the Kodokan formally treats it as if it were one. Daigo indicates that Kodokan Goshin-jutsu, and the other two[11] exercises without "-no-kata" in their names, are actually *ho* [methods]—that is, sequential groups of related techniques in a framework of principles, whose "performance" as formal demonstration was never intended. Strictly interpreting Daigo's statement yields an "official list" of seven Kodokan kata—namely Nage-no-kata, Katame-no-kata, Ju-no-kata, Go-no-kata, Kime-no-kata, Itsutu-no-kata and Koshiki-no-kata.

Earlier, the senior British judoka Syd Hoare[12] presently BJA[13] 8th dan had presented an identical viewpoint to Daigo—similarly arguing that there could be no new kata after the death of Kano, and intimating that any such creations would lack legitimacy and authority in the absence of his personal endorsement:

> From a Japanese point of view judo froze in time in 1938 when Kano died. He created Kodokan Judo which ipso facto made him the master (or *shihan*) of the school. What he created could of course be changed by him while he was still alive but not after his death… attempts to create new kata in judo have always foundered on this point.
>
> – Hoare, 2010

The Creation of Kodokan Goshin-jutsu

A New Kodokan Self-defense System

Kodokan Goshin-jutsu was formally established on 8 January 1956. Yiannakis (2002) presents Cunningham's observations on its historical origin and nature:

> The Goshin-jutsu is a construction of the 1950s, when 21 masters came together to construct a modernized form of self-defense to be taught in the Kodokan. The most influential and probably the best known to us in the West of those members was Tomiki. Kenji Tomiki had been a student of Kano and had also, by arrangement of Kano, studied under Ueshiba, of the Aikido school. Tomiki was also sent around to other of the traditional ryu, by Kano, to people that Kano knew and had made arrangements with, like Aoyagi at Sosuishi-ryu (also pronounced Sosu-ishitsu-ryu) and others. All of that old knowledge was brought to bear in the construction of the modern Goshin-jutsu. There were earlier Goshin-jutsu which are no longer practiced. They were discarded, hidden away for various reasons, and there was a feeling that there was a need for a Goshin-jutsu but the Kodokan wanted a modernized version. And so that was why they called together these instructors and asked them to construct this art. So this is designed to teach the goshin waza, whereas the Nage and Katame-no-kata teach the randori waza.
>
> – Yiannakis, 2002: 20

These remarks however are incorrect. Around 1930, Kano in fact sent two judoka—Jiro Takeda and Minoru Mochizuki[14] to study under Morihei Ueshiba (1883-1969), the eventual founder of what is now known as *aikido* [the way of unifying spirit, or, the way of spiritual harmony]. Tomiki himself had already been studying *aiki-jujutsu*[15] [the martial art of unifying spirit] directly under Ueshiba since 1926 (Shishida, 2011).

Unfortunately, Cunningham provides no specific references for his view that other Goshin-jutsu methods already existed before the war, but were subsequently concealed. One example of such an earlier method would be *Mifune Soen Goshin-jutsu* [Mifune's Personal Self-defense Techniques]—an exercise, as its name suggests, developed by Kyuzo Mifune. However, at no point was it hidden away. Mifune Soen Goshin-jutsu will be described and referenced later in this chapter when more relevant for the further content.

Relationship to Kime-no-kata

To fully understand the motivation for Kodokan Goshin-jutsu's creation, it is necessary to explore the history, position in judo, and principles of Kime-no-kata.

Kime-no-kata was intended as a kata for real combat, which was reflected in its original name—*Shinken-Shobu-no-kata* [forms of real fighting][16]. The number of techniques in the kata was initially ten, and this number was then increased to 13 or 15. The kata was later expanded again to give today's 20-technique form, and at the same time was renamed Kime-no-kata. The kata drew upon techniques from unattributed koryu jujutsu schools, as well as on Kano's own ideas.

Standardization, codification and unification of Kime-no-kata proved to be challenging, and due to a failure to agree, it was not ratified at the 24 July 1906's famous conclave of leading koryu jujutsu and judo masters held at the *Kyoto Butokuden* [Hall of Martial Virtues] of the *Dai Nippon Butokukai* (DNBK) [Greater Japan Martial Virtue Society]. Nevertheless, the Kodokan continued to use it, and eventually it was formally adopted as a *Kodokan kata* (Kano Sensei Biographic Editorial Committee, 2009: 63-65; Hoare, 2009: 62, 114-115; Kano (n.d.) cited in Watson, 2008; 79-80). However, it was never formally adopted by the DNBK.

Kime-no-kata supports the study of the theoretical basis of attack and defense. Its 20 techniques are divided into two sections—eight *idori* [kneeling] used while in *seiza* [formal seated position], and 12 *tachiai* [standing] used whilst standing. Each of these two sections contains practical and realistic defenses against empty-handed and armed attacks, and involves the safe practice of counter-attacking and control techniques prohibited from daily judo randori and shiai.

The main underlying principles for the defenses in Kime-no-kata are *tai-sabaki* [body movement][17], *shisei* [good posture], leverage and the use of *katame waza* [controlling techniques] (Kotani et al, 1968: 92-123). By understanding and developing a mastery of Kime-no-kata, one acquires the decisiveness, focus, strength of character and skills relevant to a variety of critical situations.

Kime-no-kata was formalized during the Meji period[18] but its heritage is in Edo-period[19] Japan. It therefore features defenses against typical real-world attacks from that time—including those from assailants armed with a *daisho* [literally, big-little sword set] comprising a *katana* [long, single-edged Japanese sword] and a *wakizashi* [short sword], and also those armed with a *tanto* [knife]. The Idori section of the kata reflects the scenario of a samurai visiting a *daimyo* [feudal lord] and leaving his katana at the entrance[20], but retaining his *wakizashi* and *tanto* (Carl De Crée, personal communication, 30 January 2006).

In everyday Kime-no-kata practice, a *bokken* [wooden sword] represents the katana, while a wooden[21] tanto doubles as the tanto and also the wakizashi (Ibid.). The tanto is used multiple times, in both the idori and tachiai sections, and also twice in a manner representing a wakizashi in the *kirikomi* [downward slash] attacks, both standing and seated. At some unknown time, it was deemed unnecessary to actually use two different short weapons in the kata since at the upper extreme of the tanto and the lower extreme of the wakizashi, the weapons are fairly similar in length, though the attacks with them are distinctly different. Also, the use of a tanto to represent a wakizashi simplifies the weapons handling protocol in the kata and removes the awkwardness of carrying three weapons on the tatami. When the wooden knife is being used as a tanto it is secured inside the jacket of the *judogi* [traditional uniform for judo], and when it represents a wakizashi it is secured in the belt outside the jacket.

Example techniques from Kime-no-kata are shown in the vintage photographs of Figures 1 and 2. The photographs date from the early 20th century, and are from the personal collection of one of the authors (WLG). Figure 1 shows *Ude-hishigi-hara-gatame* [arm crushing stomach armlock] from *yoko-tsuki* [side thrust] in the idori section, and Figure 2 shows *kataha-jime* [single-wing choke] from *nuki-gake* [sword unsheathing] in the tachiai section. Yoko-tsuki and nuki-gake are the eighth and eleventh techniques of the idori and tachiai sections respectively.

Figure 1 (left): *Ude-hishigi-hara-gatame* [arm crushing stomach armlock] from *yoko-tsuki* [side thrust] in the *idori* [kneeling] section of *Kime-no-kata* [forms of decisive techniques].

Figure 2 (right): *Kataha-jime* [single-wing choke] from *nukigake* [sword unsheathing] in the *tachiai* [standing] section of *Kime-no-kata* [forms of decisive techniques]. Hideichi Nagaoka is *tori* [the one demonstrating the technique] and Yoshitsugu Yamashita is *uke* [the one attacking].

The identity of the two judoka in Figure 1 is not known to the authors, but the two in Figure 2 are among the Kodokan's most distinguished judoka ever, with tori and uke[22] being respectively Hideichi Nagaoka (1876-1952) and Yoshitsugu[23] Yamashita (1865-1935). At the time both held the rank of Kodokan 7th dan, and both subsequently went on to hold the exceptional rank of Kodokan 10th dan. Most notably, Yamashita was the Kodokan's first[24] ever 10th dan holder.

Through a series of government edicts in the late nineteenth century, the open carry of swords became all but outlawed in Japan. Additionally, sitting in seiza became much less common. With these changes in lifestyle, Kime-no-kata gradually became considered outmoded for practical self-defense, and it was therefore necessary to devise a new exercise better suited to more modern circumstances. Recognizing this need, in 1952, the Kodokan established a dedicated research team (or committee) for this purpose[25].

The new exercise was to include defenses against a broader range of unarmed attacks than Kime-nokata, and also against attacks involving more contemporary weapons—specifically, a tanto, a *jo* [staff] and a *kenju* [pistol]. Attacks with the sword and short sword were discarded.

The Research Team

The Kodokan research committee charged with creating the new self defense exercise began work in September 1952. There were no less than 25 members of the team, all holding rank of 7th dan or higher, though the composition of the team did vary, both in personnel and numbers, over the time that it took to complete the task.

The names of the 25 main committee members and their historical rank (that is, at the time Kodokan Goshin-jutsu was created) are presented in Table 2 (O. Mouri, personal communication, 10 March 2014).

Table 2: The Kodokan Goshin-jutsu Research Team

Rank	Research Team Members
10th dan	Hideichi Nagaoka[26], Kyuzo Mifune, Kaichiro Samura
9th dan	Join Oda, Tamio Kurihara, Shozo Nakano
8th dan	Gensui Arai, Koki Ito, Goichi Ebii, Chu Kawakami, Yoji Kikuchi, Kazuzo Kudo, Masao Koyasu, Sumiyuki Kotani, Itsuyo Sawa, Kiyoshi Suzuki, Kisaburo Takahashi, Hamakichi Takahashi, Isao Nagahata, Masaru Hayakawa, Tadao Otaki
7th dan	Fusataro Sakamoto, Chugo Sato, Kenji Tomiki, Yoshizo Matsumoto

From Table 2 it can be seen that the theoretical and practical contribution for the development of Kodokan Goshin-jutsu came from the preeminent Kodokan teachers of the time, with three of the team, Hideichi Nagaoka[27], Kyuzo Mifune (1883-1965), and Kaichiro Samura (1880-1964), holding the rank of Kodokan 10th dan. Two of these 10th dan holders had koryu experience—specifically Nagaoka in *Kito-ryu* [school of the rise and fall] jujutsu, *Noda-ha* [Noda clan lineage], and Samura in *Takeuchi Santo-ryu jujutsu* [a now extinct koryu jujutsu style centered on the city of Kumamoto] (De Crée and Jones, 2011; C. De Crée, personal communication, 30 March 2012).

The third 10th dan holder, Mifune, had no known koryu experience, but had experimented extensively with judo's connections to both jujutsu and *torite*[28] [literally, "grasping hands"]. Despite being ideologically very different to Kano, Mifune had one of the most original and technically brilliant minds in judo. He had already contributed significantly to judo self-defense through a strong involvement in developing *Joshi Goshin Ho*, and also through the creation of *Mifune Soen Goshin-jutsu* (De Crée and Jones, 2011; De Crée, 2015).

Created sometime between 1937 and 1942, or perhaps earlier, Mifune Soen Goshin-jutsu mainly incorporates koryu and torite techniques. The exercise can be seen on a 2005-produced DVD of the famous 1955 film project—*Judo no Shinzui* [The Essence of Judo], with Mifune himself (as tori) demonstrating the techniques, and his dedicated *deshi* [student]—Sei'ichi Shirai (as uke) attacking and being defeated (Mifune, 2005). At the time of filming Mifune was 72 years old, yet still very vigorous.

Two of the team's three 9th dan holders were posthumously promoted to 10th dan—specifically Shozo Nakano (1888-1977) promoted to 10th dan in 1977, and Tamio Kurihara (1896-1979) promoted to 10th dan in 1979. One of the team's 8th dan holders was also to later achieve the rank of 10th dan—specifically Sumiyuki Kotani (1903-1991) who was promoted to that rank, during his lifetime, in 1984. Also prominent among the committee's 8th dan holders were Kazuzo Kudo[29] (1898-1970) and Tadao Otaki[30] (1908-1992)—both later promoted to 9th dan.

From the team, it is Kotani (Figure 3) and Tomiki (Figure 4) who arguably became the greatest and best-known experts of Kodokan Goshin-jutsu. Kotani's personal performance of the exercise was known to be very impressive—particularly his *tekubi-waza* [wrist techniques]. A rare color recording of him performing Kodokan Goshin-jutsu does exist—though, to date, it has not been made available on modern media.

As well as having a very high level of personal proficiency, Tomiki's contribution to the development of Kodokan Goshin-jutsu was particularly significant, and will be detailed now.

Figure 3 (left): Sumiyuki Kotani (1903-1991).
Figure 4 (right): Kenji Tomiki (1900-1979).

Role and Contribution of Kenji Tomiki

The name from the research team that is most closely associated with the formulation of Kodokan Goshin-jutsu is undoubtedly Kenji Tomiki (1900-1979). He wrote the first and most important textbook on the exercise—*Kodokan Goshin-jutsu* (Tomiki, 1958), Figure 5, and also the slightly earlier and highly original book, *Judo, Appendix: Aikido* later renamed *Judo and Aikido* (Tomiki, 1956; 1967). *Judo, Appendix: Aikido*, Figure 6, explains how judo and aikido complement each other, with the book's aikido appendix being among the earliest English language text on that system.

Figure 5 (left): *Kodokan Goshin-jutsu* by Kenji Tomiki was published in 1958 and was the first textbook on the exercise.
Figure 6 (right): *Judo, Appendix: Aikido* by Kenji Tomiki was published in 1956 and takes a highly original approach to both styles.

Tomiki was born on 15 March 1900 in Kakunodate, Akita Prefecture. He was one of the earliest students of Morihei Ueshiba, and also a direct student of Kano-shihan. A graduate of the Political Economic Department of Waseda University[31], Tomiki later became Professor of Calligraphy, and also head of the Physical Education Department, at his alma marter. Additionally, he was a member of the Kodokan's Special Direction Committee and an official of the All Japan Judo Federation. Tomiki was also central to continuing and executing some of the theoretical work to reinforce the martial aspects of judo that Kano started to reconsider near the end of his life[32]. Shishida (2010; 2011; 2012; 2013) describes a number of these plans.

In a formative article in the development of Kodokan Goshin-jutsu, Tomiki (1953) explored the relationships between judo as a martial art, as self-defense, and as a restricted subset of koryu jujutsu. Some of the key themes in this chapter will now be presented as they provide important background context to Tomiki's contribution to Kodokan Goshin-jutsu.

Originally, koryu jujutsu schools taught a broad range of techniques, including many of those in the *bugei juhappan* [the "traditional" eighteen martial arts] that every samurai should know[33]. These arts include *so-jutsu* [art of spear], *naginata-jutsu* [art of halberd], *kyu-jutsu* [archery], *ken-jutsu* [art of sword], *bo-jutsu* [art of staff], *jo-jutsu* [art of short staff], even *ba-jutsu* [martial horse-riding] and *sui-jutsu* [combative swimming].

Examples of schools, still extant, that would teach such a large number of armed and unarmed techniques today include *Takeuchi-ryu* [one of the oldest koryu schools founded by Hisamori Takenouchi who instituted the school during the late Muromachi period], *Araki-ryu* [believed to have been founded by Araki Muninsai, and originally taught in the area near modern Nagoya] and *Sosuishitsu-ryu* [School of Grasping the Two Waters]. These are known as *sogo bujutsu* [integrated or comprehensive martial arts] as opposed to a single purpose school like archery or swordsmanship.

Koryu jujutsu's techniques include those for situations such as when gripping one's opponent [*kumu*]—throwing, pinning, choking, and crushing; those for when separated and not gripping one's opponent—striking, thrusting, and kicking; those for when unarmed and facing an armed opponent—defending against strikes with sword, spear, staff, and finally those for when armed—using weapons such as sword, spear and staff. In his judo, Kano restricted koryu's multiple complex techniques in favor of throwing and grappling techniques, with striking techniques being restricted to kata.

In his seminal article, Tomiki highlighted that there are two methods of ensuring that an attacker's violence cannot be directed against oneself—simply to injure, or not to injure, the adversary. Tomiki also emphasized that there are two types of joint techniques—the first type being direct attacks to vulnerable areas for inflicting, or threatening to inflict damage to the adversary's joints, and the second type being indirect attacks against mechanically vulnerable areas to destroy the assailant's balance. Furthermore, Tomiki highlighted that there are two ways of considering atemi-waza. First, as techniques used against the opponent's physiological weak points [*kyusho*] to injure or kill them, and secondly as techniques used against his biomechanical weak points to take his balance [*kuzushi*] and throw him.

Tomiki's innovative concept was to use judo for close range, and aikido from at a distance, and while there is no direct mention of Kodokan Goshin-jutsu in the text of *Judo, Appendix: Aikido*, there is content very closely associated with it. Unsurprisingly, this material is found in the aikido appendix, alongside some of the ideas presented in the 1953 article (Tomiki, 1956; 1967: 101-180). For example, Figure 7 shows Tomiki executing defenses against an attacker armed with a pistol (Ibid.: 166-167). These have clearly been incorporated, albeit in a slightly modified form, into Kodokan Goshin-jutsu (Ibid.: 170-171).

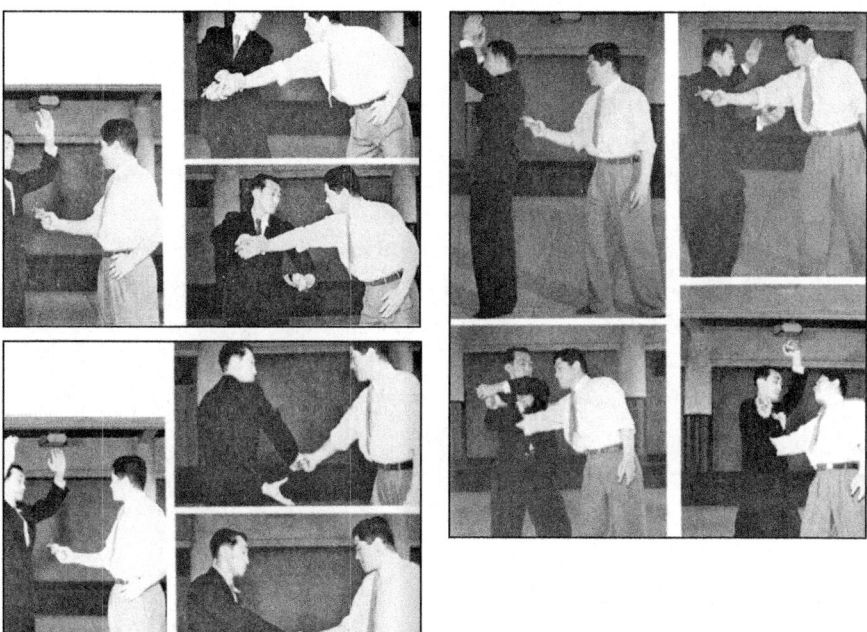

Figure 7: Kenji Tomiki showing a number of aikido defenses against an attacker armed with a pistol. From his own book, *Judo Appendix Aikido*.

Tomiki's role in developing Kodokan Goshin-jutsu is often overstated, particularly by Western authors, with many incorrectly suggesting that either he would have personally created, or compiled, the exercise, or else would have been the Chairman of the committee that did so. In 1956 when Kodokan Goshin-jutsu was established, Tomiki held the judo rank of Kodokan 7th dan, and the *aiki-budo*[34] [the martial way of unifying spirit] rank of 8th dan[35]. Tomiki was not the committee Chairman, since at the time, six of its members were 9th or 10th dan holders, with 15 others holding 8th dan, and all therefore senior to him. Given the strong hierarchical structure of Japanese society, protocol and respect for seniority would have made Nagaoka, Mifune and Samura the leaders.

Notwithstanding, Tomiki was a major technical contributor to the development of Kodokan Goshin-jutsu—providing, in particular, a very strong aiki-jujutsu input. Risei Kano (1900-1986), the (third) Kodokan Kancho from 1946 to 1980 (and the Shihan's son) specifically highlighted Tomiki's contribution in his preface to the original 1958 Kodokan Goshin-jutsu textbook. Originally in Japanese:

> Kano-shihan made every effort possible to complete judo as a modern physical education, but could not yet systematize the self-defense aspect of judo which is contained in classical jujutsu, even though he did study it deeply. That he was very much concerned about the self-defense aspect of judo is clearly seen from the fact that he sent some of his students to Ueshiba-sensei to study aiki-jujutsu, and also invited an expert on jo-jutsu to the Kodokan for a seminar. Some of the self-defense techniques are incorporated into Kime-no-kata which is well known to all. After WWII, quite a few judoka abroad showed interest in the self-defense aspect of judo, and the Kodokan organized a panel to create and publish the Kodokan Goshin-jutsu. As stated earlier, since the Kodokan had already started its study, it was fairly easy to reach consensus. The writer of this book, Professor Kenji Tomiki has deep understanding of judo as a Professor at Waseda University and also as an authority on research of aikijutsu in the light of judo principles. In formulating Goshin-jutsu, he played a leading role in the panel. I am firmly convinced, therefore, that this book will become the best guidebook for all practitioners of judo self-defense.
>
> Risei Kano, December 1958
> – Tomiki, 1958: 3-4

Additionally, Tomiki was tori in the first public demonstration of Kodokan Goshin-jutsu during the Kagami Biraki ceremony held at the Tokyo Budokan in January 1956. His fellow committee-member, Otaki, was uke. In this demonstration, Kodokan Goshin-jutsu was shown as an unceremonial and practical self-defense method based on judo principles, rather than a formal kata[36]. Highlights from this demonstration can be seen on the DVD *Classic Judo Kata* edited by Hal Sharp[37] (2013), and also on the most recent DVD release of the Kodokan-produced Kodokan Goshin-jutsu instructional film (Kodokan, 2009)—see later.

Tomiki was promoted to the judo rank of Kodokan 8th dan in 1971, and died on 25 December 1979. He was 79 years old.

STRUCTURE AND TECHNICAL CONTENTS OF KODOKAN GOSHIN-JUTSU

The Name Kodokan Goshin-jutsu

Goshin-jutsu means "self-defense", and is merely a set of applications that can be used in conflict situations. The inclusion of the term "-jutsu" does not imply that Kodokan Goshin-jutsu is part of *bujutsu*[38] [martial art/science]—it is of course part of judo, a martial way [*budo*[39]], where there is greater emphasis on principles and educational aspects, than on the use of techniques in actual combat.

Tomiki explains, in a matter-of-fact way, why "Kodokan" was affixed to the title of the new exercise. Over the first 38 pages of the original Kodokan Goshin-jutsu textbook (Tomiki, 1958), he emphasizes that judo self-defense must be a practical application of judo techniques that are derived from judo principles. In so doing, Tomiki is placing Kodokan Goshin-jutsu firmly within the context of judo, and is primarily for this reason that today the exercise is regarded as a member of the Kodokan kata family.

Including the word "Kodokan" as a prefix was natural, as it clearly differentiated the new exercise from the archaic Kime-no-kata. Whereas in Kime-no-kata one could maim, or kill, an attacker, Kodokan Goshin-jutsu was a more modern adjunct for self-defense purposes only. Kodokan Goshin-jutsu was also designed to be consistent with a core principle of judo, namely *seiryoku zen'yo*, with its aim being not to damage or punish an attacker, but to immobilize or incapacitate them, so that no further attack was possible (Cornish, 1984: 7).

Past Names for Kodokan Goshin-jutsu

Kodokan Goshin-jutsu has, in the past, been infrequently referred to by two other names—*Ippan-yo Goshin-no-kata* [Regular Use Self Defense Forms] and *Shin-Kime-no-kata* [New Kime-no-kata].

Ippan-yo Goshin-no-kata

The opening paragraph of Chapter X, "General Description of the Prearranged Forms of Judo" in the text *Illustrated Kodokan Judo* mentions for the first time a self-defense kata called *Ippan-yo Goshin-no-kata* [Regular Use Self-Defense Forms]:

> There are nine kinds of Kata or forms generally taught today at Kodokan. They are... (3) *Kime-no-kata* (Forms of Decision) or Shinken-shobu-no-Kata (Forms of Actual Fighting)...(8) *Fujoshi-yo-Goshin-no-Kata* (Forms of Self-Defence for Girls and Women); and (9) *Ippan-yo Goshin-no-Kata* (Forms of Self-Defence for Men).
> – Kodokan, 1955: 161

Ippan-yo-Goshin-no-kata was the unofficial temporary designation ("working title") for Kodokan Goshin-jutsu during its development phase, which by when *Illustrated Kodokan Judo* was first published in 1955, was almost at an end. It is not known why Ippan-yo Goshin-no-kata was wrongly translated in the book as "Forms of Self-Defence for Men", though it can be speculated that the erroneous inclusion of the phrase "for Men" could have been an attempt to distinguish it from the self-defense exercises for women, which, through Joshi Goshin Ho[40] had been available since 1943. The inclusion of the phrase "Regular Use" in the proper translation suggests that the exercise was intended for the general public, and not just for professionals like security operatives, law enforcement officers and other individuals working in high-risk environments.

Mikinosuke Kawaishi (1899-1970) DNBK / Kodokan 7th dan, FFJDA[41] 10th dan[42] mentions similar self-defense kata in his significant book[43] *The Complete 7 Katas of Judo*:

> At the Kodokan they still study the Seiryoku-zenyo-kokumin-taiku-no-kata, or Kata of Physical Training, and also two derived from the Kime-no-kata, a Kata of Defence for Women and another a little different for Men.
> – Kawaishi, 1957: 11

While the Japanese names of these two other self-defense kata is omitted, the clear parallels between Kawaishi's text and that previously cited, would suggest that they are Joshi Goshin Ho and Ippan-yo Goshin-nokata respectively.

Inexplicably, Ippan-yo Goshin-no-kata continues to be mentioned in the later and expanded (299 pages cf. 285), reprint of *Illustrated Kodokan Judo*. This is despite Kodokan Goshin-jutsu having by then been established for 20 years, summarized in Chapter X[44] (Kodokan, 1976: 163), and described in detail in Chapter XIV (Ibid.: 209-216).

> There are nine kinds of Kata or forms generally taught today at Kodokan. They are.... (3) *Kime-no-kata* (Forms of Decision) or *Shinken-shobu-no-Kata* (Forms of Actual Fighting); (4) *Kodokan-Goshin-jutsu* (Forms of Self-Defence)... (9) *Fujoshi-yo-Goshin-no-Kata* (Forms of Self-Defence for Girls and Women); and (10) *Ippan-yo Goshin-no-Kata* (Forms of Self-Defence for Men).
>
> – Ibid.: 161

The statement "There are nine kinds of Kata..." with the subsequent listing of ten exercises indicates editorial quality control shortcomings with the reprint. Beyond this error, by separately numbering Ippan-yo-Goshin-no-kata and Kodokan Goshin-jutsu, the reprint is implying that they are different exercises, which, as already explained, is incorrect. Additionally, inserting Kodokan Goshin-jutsu into fourth position in the list, instead of being appended at the end, is an error and source of confusion, as it causes the other, and earlier, Kodokan kata to be wrongly ordered.

Note that the 1986 revised and update version of *Illustrated Kodokan Judo*, published by Kodansha under the simple title of *Kodokan Judo* (Kano[45], 1986), makes no mention of Ippan-yo Goshin-no-kata. This reliably establishes the obsolescence of this 1950s interim designation and the discontinuation of its use.

The final named mention of Ippan-yo Goshin-no-kata in the literature is in Cunningham's wide-ranging interview with Yiannakis. Therein, Yiannakis remarks:

> There are other kata which are not currently recognized by the Kodokan, such as Go no Kata, Ippon Yo Goshin-jutsu no Kata [sic], Gonosen no Kata, and others. What are the origins and nature of these so-called "lost kata" and why do you think they are no longer widely known?
>
> – Yiannakis, 2003: 20

Cunningham responds:

> As for the other kata, for example, there were earlier Goshin Jutsu. There was Ippon Yo Goshin Jutsu no Kata [sic] and Fujoshi Goshin-jutsu no Kata. Ippon Yo Goshin-jutsu no Kata—*ippon yo* means "general; it's the general self defense art that was taught to everybody. There had to be some place to learn all the goshin waza, which was the other half of judo. You have randori waza and goshin waza, and if you're going to teach the full syllabus, you have to teach both.

There was also Fujoshi Goshin-jutsu no Kata, which was the women's version. What it really meant was that it was the techniques which are special to women's attacks. It focused on those specifically. These two kata, like the Go no Kata, were sort of lost before WWII, quite deliberately I think, and the loss of them gave rise to the Joshi Goshinho and Kime Shiki that appeared in the Women's Division during WWII, and the new Goshin Jutsu which appeared in the 1950s as a result of the research group that I mentioned earlier.

– Ibid.: 20

Cunningham does not provide any references for his view that Ippon Yo Goshin Jutsu no Kata [sic] was an early self-defense form, and that it, together with some other kata such as Go-no-kata, were lost pre-war. Moreover, there are several material errors in his answer to Yiannakis. First, Kime Shiki pre-dates Joshi Goshin Ho by a decade or more. Next, while it is correct that Go-no-kata is seldom taught or practiced today, it is not "lost" having been preserved mainly by the efforts of the late Yoshiyuki Kuhara (1906-1985) Kodokan 9th dan and his nephew Toshiyasu Ochiai, presently Kodokan 8th dan (De Crée and Jones, 2009; Ochiai, 2012). Finally, as already explained, Ippan-yo Goshin-no-kata was merely Kodokan Goshin-jutsu's working title, and so clearly post-war. Given the litany of errors in this answer, Cunningham's observations on Ippan-yo Goshin-no-kata should be discarded.

Shin-Kime-no-kata
The kata books written by Sumiyuki Kotani, in combination with various other authors, have long been a reference text for serious judoka. One of the most detailed treatments of Kodokan Goshin-jutsu is contained in the book *Kata of Kodokan Judo*, and its reprint, the *Kata of Kodokan Judo Revised* (Kotani et al, 1968: 54-91):

Kodokan Goshinjitsu [sic.] is the new form formulated by Kodokan Judo Institute in January 1956 and is composed of, as its name manifests, 21 techniques suitable for defending ourselves from unexpected attacks of others...

... It may be called as *Shin-Kime-no-kata* (New Forms of Self-defense).

– Ibid.: 54

Similarly, John Cornish[46], in his detailed booklet on Kodokan Goshin-jutsu writes:

The Go-shin-jutsu is sometimes called the *Shin* (new) Kime-no-kata, and as it contains different defence moves from those in Kime-no-kata, even where the attack is the same, it can be thought of as an addition to Kime-nokata.
– Cornish, 1984: 3

Additionally, Daigo's previously mentioned lecture note presents a brief overview of Kodokan Goshin-jutsu, together with some of its history. This material is a translated excerpt from Kotani and Otaki (1971):

This kata was made at Showa 31 (January 1956). It is almost the same as Kime no kata. It should be called *Shin kime no kata* (New Kime no kata).
– Kotani and Otaki, 1971 cited in Daigo, 2008)

Notwithstanding these references from senior judoka, the name Shin-Kime-no-kata, although sometimes heard, was never officially in use, and so should be discarded.

Etiquette in Kodokan Goshin-jutsu

The *reiho*[47] [etiquette] in Kodokan Goshin-jutsu, has tori standing with *joseki* [seat of seniority] to his right. This is a reversal of the positions in the more basic, Randori-no-kata, but identical to those in Ju-no-kata. After the initial standing bow, uke turns through 90° to face *joseki*, walks forwards, kneels in seiza and then places the weapons on the *tatami* [mat]—see Figure 8. Uke then returns to his original position and stands facing tori. Both tori and uke then step forward into *shizen-hontai* [basic natural posture] ready to begin.

Note that the reiho within Kodokan Goshin-jutsu has changed over time. Originally, a seated bowing ceremony was featured, and then for an interim period, either a sitting or a standing bow[48] was accepted. Finally, normalization of Kodokan Goshin-jutsu standards resulted in the standing bowing ceremony that is always seen today.

Figure 8: Etiquette in Kodokan Goshin-jutsu shown by Masaru Sato.

Technical Contents of Kodokan Goshin-jutsu

A schematic overview of the structure and contents of Kodokan Goshin-jutsu is presented in Table 3 where it can be seen that the exercise is divided into two main sections—each containing defenses against distinct and differentiated attack types—*toshi-no-bu* [unarmed attacks] and *Buki-no-bu* [armed attacks].

Table 3: Structural and Functional Overview of Kodokan Goshin-jutsu

Kodokan Goshin-jutsu [Kodokan Self-defense]

Toshu-no-bu [unarmed attacks]	
Kumitsu-kareta-baai [When held]	Hanareta-baai [When attacked from a distance]
1. Ryote-dori [Two-hand hold] 2. Hidari-eri-dori [Left-lapel hold] 3. Migi-eri-dori [Right-lapel hold] 4. Kataude-dori [Single-hand hold] 5. Ushiro-eri-dori [Collar hold from behind] 6. Ushiro-jime [Choke from behind] 7. Kakae-dori [Seize and hold from behind]	1. Naname-uchi [Slanting strike] 2. Ago-tsuki [Uppercut] 3. Gammen-tsuki [Thrust-punch to face] 4. Mae-geri [Front kick] 5. Yoko-geri [Side kick]

Buki-no-bu [armed attacks]		
Tanto-no-baai [knife attacks]	Tsue-no-baai [staff attacks]	Kenju-no-baai [pistol attacks]
1. Tsukkake [thrust] 2. Choku-tsuki [straight thrust] 3. Naname-tsuki [slanting stab]	1. Furiage [upswing] 2. Furi-oroshi [downswing] 3. Morote-tsuki [two-hand thrust]	1. Shomen-zuke [at the front] 2. Koshi-gamae [held on hip] 3. Haimen-zuke [at the back]

Vocals	
By Uke	By Tori
Kiai for all atemi-waza "Te wo ageru" for all Kenshu-no-bai	Kiai for all atemi-waza

The names of the individual attacks themselves follow an established and highly efficient naming convention, as described by Cornish:

> The Japanese names used for the techniques in the kata only describe parts of the attack. To use a comprehensive description of all the attack and the defence would make the name too long-winded and, for the non-Japanese, difficult to remember whereas these short names should prove no difficulty at all. The English…is not meant to be a transcription of the Japanese names, like them it is meant only as a memory aid.
> – Ibid.; 3

The Toshu-no-bu section contains 12 attacks, split into two subsections. The first one, called *Kumitsukareta-baai*, consists of seven attacks from an assailant that one is already in contact with, or who is close by. The second, called *Hanareta-baai*, contains five attacks at a distance, with the attacker suddenly coming in from afar. Example techniques from Toshu-no-bu are shown in Figures 9a and 9b. Specifically, Figure 9a shows *Kote-hineri* [wrist twist] from *Ryote-dori* [two hand-hold] and Figure 9b shows *osoto-otoshi* [major outer drop twist] from *naname-uchi* [slanting strike]. Recall from Table 3 that Ryote-dori and naname-uchi are the first attacks in the Kumitsu-kareta-baai and Hanareta-baai subsections respectively.

Figure 9a (left): *Kote-hineri* [wrist twist] from *ryote-dori* [two hand-hold] in the *toshi-no-bu* [unarmed attacks] section.
Figure 9b (right): *Osoto-otoshi* [major outer drop twist] from *naname-uchi* [slanting strike] in the *toshi-no-bu* [unarmed attacks] section.

The Buki-no-bu section contains nine named attacks, split into three subsections, of three attacks each. The first subsection, named Tanto-no-baai comprises three knife attacks. The second, named Tsue-no-baai comprises three staff attacks. The third, named Kenju-no-baai comprises three pistol attacks. Example techniques from Buki-no-bu are shown in Figures 10a, 10b and 10c. Figure 10a shows tori taking away uke's knife from *naname-tsuki* [slanting stab], Figure 10b shows tori throwing uke down from *furi-oroshi* [downswing], and Figure 10c shows tori throwing uke from *haimen-zuke* [pistol at the back]. Again, recall from Table 3 that naname-tsuki is the third attack in the Tanto-no-baai subsection, furi-oroshi is the second attack in the Tsue-no-baai subsection and Haimen-zuke is the third attack in the Kenju-no-baai subsection.

Figure 10a (left): Taking away the knife from *naname-tsuki* [slanting stab] in the *Buki-no-bu* [armed attacks] section.

Figure 10b (center): Throwing uke down from *furi-oroshi* [downswing] in the *Buki-no-bu* [armed attacks] section.

Figure 10c (right): Throwing uke down from *haimen-zuke* [pistol at the back] in the *Buki-no-bu* [armed attacks] section.

The photographs of Figures 9a to 10c are from the Kodokan Goshin-jutsu performance at the 2002 Kodokan Kagami Biraki. Tsueno Sengoku presently Kodokan 8th dan is tori [the one demonstrating the technique] and Masaru Sato presently Kodokan 8th dan is uke [the one attacking].

To date, the Kodokan has reviewed the Kodokan Goshin-jutsu three times since its inception—in July 1987, in December 1992 and in July 2004. The July 1987 review by the Kodokan's Kodokan Goshin-jutsu Research Committee, chaired by Kotani, was the most extensive and significant and was aimed at unifying and standardizing the exercise. This included clarifying many of its key technical points, the protocol for handling the weapons and the positioning of tori and uke. Following the review, a new Kodokan teaching booklet was published (Kodokan, 1987).

Foundations of Kodokan Goshin-jutsu

The composition and structure of Kodokan Goshin-jutsu was influenced by that of the other Kodokan kata, which, in their finalized form, contain either 15 techniques—Nage-no-kata, Katame-no-kata and Ju-no-kata, or 20-21 techniques—Kime-no-kata and Koshiki-no-kata. Note that although Go-no-kata and Itsutsu-no-kata only contain ten and five techniques, respectively, both these kata were unfinished by Kano, and most likely would have been later revised and expanded to include more techniques.

The division of Kodokan Goshin-jutsu into unarmed and armed sections was logical, and the number of attacks in each section was of course initially arbitrary. However, some underlying structural logic was necessary, and the armed section eventually followed a similar pattern to Kime-no-kata, with equal number of attacks per weapons type. Under this approach, having two attacks per weapon-type produced a total of six defense sequences, and having three, produced nine. This would leave either 12 or 15 attacks available for the unarmed section. The structuring of this into subsections for "when held" and "at a distance" would, due to Tomiki's influence, come later.

As well as introducing new attack types into judo, Kodokan Goshin-jutsu also preserved, and built upon, a number of attack forms already contained in Kime-no-kata[49] and, to a much lesser degree, in Ju-no-kata[50]. As part of updating Kime-no-kata, the attacks in Kodokan Goshin-jutsu were however usually executed in a modified way, or on a different side. Kodokan Goshin-jutsu also introduced alternative defenses. Table 4 lists the similar attacks found in Kime-no-kata and Kodokan Goshin-jutsu.

Figure 4: Similar Attacks in Kime-no-kata and Kodokan Goshin-jutsu		
Attack	Kime-no-kata (Tachiai Section)	Kodokan Goshin-jutsu
Two-hand hold	Ryote-dori	Ryote-dori
Single-hand (sleeve) hold	Sode-dori	Kataude-dori
Hold from behind	Ushiro-dori	Kakae-dori
Single-fist thrust punch	Tsukkake	Ganmen-tsuki
Uppercut	Tsuki-age	Ago-tsuki
Front kick	Ke-age	Mae-geri

As an example, consider Ryote-dori. In Kime-no-kata this attack concludes with tori applying a *katame waza* [controlling technique]—specifically the *kansetsu-waza* [joint-locking technique] *ude-hishigi-waki-gatame* [arm crushing armpit armlock] against uke's left arm. Kodokan Goshin-jutsu provides tori with an additional method for freeing his right wrist, and concludes with him applying a different kansetsu-waza—this time *Kote-hineri* [wrist twist] against uke's right arm.

Another example is the attack comprising a single-fist thrust punch to the face. This attack is known as *tsukkake* in the tachiai section of Kime-no-kata, and Ganmen-tsuki in Kodokan Goshin-jutsu. In both exercises the attack concludes with tori applying a katame waza—specifically the same *shime-waza* [strangulation technique] *hadaka-jime* [naked choke] in both cases.

PRINCIPLES WITHIN KODOKAN GOSHIN-JUTSU

The central objective in Kodokan Goshin-jutsu is to use judo self-defense principles to defeat an adversary and survive. Every defense in the exercise has fundamental principles for its effective execution, and in learning the exercise, it is these principles that have to be understood and mastered. However, in English-language texts on Kodokan Goshin-jutsu, it is only Kotani et al, (1968: 54-91) and Cornish (1984) that pay proper attention to the principles as being the exercise's most vital aspect. Hopefully, one of the contributions of the current chapter will be to further an understanding of these principles, by assisting in making them more accessible to the interested judoka.

Self-Confidence and Focus

What matters most in any self-defense situation is the individual, and their personal ability to handle real life conflict, both physically and emotionally. For this reason, it is largely irrelevant what bujutsu, budo, or even combat sport one has studied. Remaining composed, under stress, is more important for self-defense than being technically skilled, or physically in good condition. This is because if an individual cannot control their own mind, their potential for being able to control another person is similarly limited.

Kotani *et al* highlight the role of Kodokan Goshin-jutsu in fostering self-confidence:

> ... practice of Goshinjitsu [sic.] aims to acquire the techniques and the self-confidence which can be applied effectively and timely for defending ourselves from unexpected attacks of others...
> – Kotani et al, 1968: 57

Through practicing Kodokan Goshin-jutsu, tori develops decisiveness and the confidence to use tai-sabaki to quickly get into the correct position to parry attacks and execute defenses—depending on the *maai*[51] [interval or spacing] and *debana* [opportunity]. Practice also helps foster mental capabilities through furthering *mushin*[52] [no-mindedness] and *zanshin*[53] [awareness (in case of further attacks)]. Both aspects improve as tori becomes more proficient in executing Kodokan Goshin-jutsu's various defenses, and begins using them against a variety of random attacks such as those shown in Cornish (1984: 30-32).

Kuzushi

The most critical technical principle in Kodokan Goshin-jutsu is *kuzushi* [balance breaking], with the aim being to create a safe opportunity for tori to counter-attack, and ultimately control uke. Without kuzushi, tori cannot easily achieve the necessary control, and in such circumstances, the defenses become unrealistic and even dangerous for tori to attempt. This is because a uke that is not unbalanced can simultaneously counter-attack tori.

The original informal Kodokan Goshin-jutsu was a great training in kuzushi, due mainly to Tomiki's contribution, however, over the years that focus has been largely lost. Proper practice of Kodokan Goshin-jutsu helps teach tori kuzushi skills for use in non-sports competitive judo situations —including against an armed attacker, where it is impossible, or very difficult, to grip uke and perform basic *Happo-no-Kuzushi* [eight directions of unbalancing] (Cornish, 1984: 7).

Kodokan Goshin-jutsu teaches tori how to use both indirect, and direct action to generate kuzushi. Tori's indirect actions mainly involve correct tai-sabaki, with him moving and repositioning his whole body. Tori's direct actions often involve *atemi-waza* [striking techniques][54] to provide kuzushi— prior to applying a decisive technique such as a *nage-waza* [throwing technique] or katame waza. Direct action using atemi-waza is also used to create mental kuzushi—where it is uke's concentration, more than his body that is disturbed. This distraction produces an instantaneous opportunity for tori to counter-attack.

Execution of Technique in a Dynamic Situation

Kodokan Goshin-jutsu introduces the concept of dynamic displacement into judo self-defense, with its attacks and defenses being executed from moving situations. This contrasts with the predominantly static situations in Kime-no-kata. Against uke's attacks, tori must quickly use tai-sabaki to prepare his movements and get into the correct position to control or throw uke. In so doing, it is vital that tori maintains control of his own balance and posture, while moving himself, and controlling uke.

Controlling Distance

Kodokan Goshin-jutsu exposes judoka to the combat principles that result from working with an increased maai compared to that normally found in everyday judo including the other Kodokan kata. In particular, the maai in the Toshu-no-bu section is significantly greater than that in ordinary judo randori, and the use of weapons in the Buki-no-bu section increases the maai even further.

The Kumitsu-kareta-baai and Hanareta-baai subsections of the Toshu-no-bu in Kodokan Goshin-jutsu teach very different principles from Kime-no-kata. Whereas in Kime-no-kata, tori and uke are in a fixed, close-in, positions, and there are no real attacks from distance[55], the Hanareta-baai subsection of Kodokan Goshin-jutsu specifically teaches tori how to cope with attacks from an assailant suddenly coming in from afar. Note that it is the scenarios where there is some distance between tori and uke, that Tomiki made his greatest contribution—not just to Kodokan Goshin-jutsu, but to judo as a whole (Tomiki, 1956; Shishida, 2010; 2011).

Proper Use of Leverage

The effective use of leverage is an essential element of most of the defenses in Kodokan Goshin-jutsu. Through practice, tori learns how leverage can be effectively applied to different components of uke's body, depending upon the actual defense being executed, and both his own and uke's movements.

Defense Against a Pistol

Kodokan Goshin-jutsu introduces, for the first time, the concept of defenses against guns into formal Kodokan training, and hence judo. In the Kenshu-no-bai scenarios, uke threatens tori with a pistol to gain compliance and take his wallet. Uke has no real set intention of shooting tori, but the scenario is that he might do so if compliance is not forthcoming.

A critical point in the gun attack scenarios is that uke looks down as he reaches for tori's wallet. This break in focus provides tori with the opportunity to take the initiative, move out of the line of fire, and counter-attack. Uke's brain must first register that tori has moved, and subsequently must process a decision whether, or not, to pull the trigger. Action beats reaction, and providing his hands are held up at shoulder height, and not above his head, tori should have sufficient time to control the gun and disarm uke.

The Kenshu-no-bai subsection therefore introduces new principles into judo that are not found elsewhere. Most important is the principle that tori only starts to counter-attack, when uke's attention is not on him. Taisabaki is critical, and tori must have turned to always have his own body out of the gun's line of fire. Also, tori must always attack the hand holding the gun, or the gun itself, seizing the barrel, warding it off, and using it as a lever to disarm or throw uke.

The principles which are *sine quo non* for the Kenshu-no-baai are very well illustrated in the third gun attack—*haimen-zuke*. This is not only the last attack of the Kenshu-no-baai, but also the final attack of the entire Kodokan Goshin-jutsu.

In haimen-zuke, uke is standing behind tori, and as tori walks forwards, uke follows. Drawing the pistol with his right hand uke commands *"Te wo ageru"* ["hands up"]. Tori stops and slowly complies. Uke then steps forward with his right foot, places the pistol muzzle against the middle of tori's back, and reaches for tori's wallet. During this time tori has already glanced out of the corner of his eye to see which of uke's arms has the gun.

As uke reaches down to tori's pocket for the wallet, tori uses tai-sabaki by slightly lowering his hips and turning to his right, dropping his right hand under uke's gun hand as he does so. Tori then raises his hand up and over, catching his right forearm in the crook of uke's arm in the process. Tori then pulls forward and uses pressure to trap uke's right (gun) arm. Subsequently, tori disarms uke by capturing the gun with his other (left) hand.

In Tomiki's original text (1958) haimen-zuke concludes here, with tori being poised to strike uke in the head with the gun. This ending is consistent with the two preceding pistol defenses that finish in a similar manner. The photographic sequence of Figure 11 shows this original form, with Tomiki as tori and Mr. Sakamoto of Waseda University as uke (Tomiki, 1958).

Figure 11: The original form of *haimen-zuke* [pistol at the back] the final technique of Kodokan-Goshin-jutsu concluding with tori simply disarming uke. Kenji Tomiki is tori [the one demonstrating the technique] and Mr. Sakamoto is uke [the one attacking].

However, in quite short order, a modified ending to haimen-zuke started to feature, with tori throwing uke to the ground using a *kote-gaeshi* [wrist reversal] type technique. The first documented example of this (known to the authors) actually has Tomiki himself as tori, and features in the book *Judo*

(Kodokan, 1961) which was published in 1961 to mark the centenary of Jigoro Kano's birth. Most interestingly, while the photographs in the book clearly show tori throwing uke, the supporting text makes no mention of the throw and only refers to tori disarming uke. Similarly, in the book *Saishin Judo-no-Kata Zen* [*The Latest Judo Kata—Complete*] (Kotani and Otaki, 1971) a throw is shown in the photographs without any supporting text. This is not unusual as in Japanese-authored books the text always takes precedence over any photographs. The photographic sequence of Figure 12 shows this modified form of haimen-zuke, with Tomiki as tori, and his close friend and colleague Hideo Oba (1910-1986) Kodokan 6th dan, aikido 9th dan, as uke (Kodokan, 1961).

Figure 12: The modified form of *haimen-zuke* [pistol at the back] the final technique of Kodokan-Goshin-jutsu concluding with tori throwing uke with a *kote-gaeshi* [wrist reversal] style technique. Kenji Tomiki is tori [the one demonstrating the technique] and Hideo Oba is uke [the one attacking].

Note that where most texts consider only one of the endings to haimen-zuke, the 2007 book *Judo Kata—Les Formes Classiques du Kodokan* by Inogai[56] and Habersetzer[57], considers both. While the illustrations only show the throw, the narrative (originally in French) states:

> Tori may seek not to throw [uke]: he can simply seize the gun with his left hand and then strike the back of uke's head with the butt, remaining standing and simply leaning forward slightly.
> The same as in the previous two techniques.
> – Inogai and Habersetzer, 2007: 208

Whilst it might be assumed that making a significant modification to Kodokan Goshin-jutsu, such as introducing a throw into haimen-zuke, would have been the subject of extensive debate amongst Kodokan seniors, it seems that this change became assimilated through informal practice, and only officially sanctioned once it was established as the norm.

The possibility of having two different concluding techniques for haimen-zuke is of course entirely consistent with the philosophy for Kodokan Goshin-jutsu, and indeed all of judo. Core principles have to be followed throughout, but the application of those principles is permitted to vary. Accordingly, the absence, or presence, of the concluding throw in haimen-zuke is of limited relevance, since from a self-defense perspective, both endings are valid, and there is no compelling reason why uke has to be thrown in the way he is today.

It was only in the mid-1980s that the Kodokan's "Kodokan Goshin-jutsu Research Committee" formally decided that uke should be thrown after tori had snatched the pistol. Naturally, it was only after the taking of this decision that authoritative Kodokan Goshin-jutsu teaching material began including both photographs showing, and text describing, haimen-zuke culminating with a throw.

Sequential Self-defense

The greatest insight into Kodokan Goshin-jutsu is obtained by considering it as containing 21 self-defense "sequences" as opposed 21 distinct "techniques". These sequences are significantly more complex than those found in everyday randori and sports competition judo, and involve, *inter alia*, atemi-waza, tai-sabaki, kuzushi, nage-waza and katame waza, for which a limitless number of permutations and combinations exist.

This complexity of the sequences in Kodokan Goshin-jutsu is now illustrated by considering the first defense, Ryote-dori. As soon as uke reaches the proper maai, he steps forwards, grasps both of tori's wrists and attacks tori's groin [*kokan*] with an atemi-waza—*hiza-ate* [knee strike] using his right knee. Tori cannot block or deflect, this incoming knee, so he responds logically with tai-sabaki—evading the attack, by stepping back with his left foot, turning slightly to the left and taking uke's balance—kuzushi.

Simultaneously, tori breaks free from uke's left-hand grip by using leverage and stretching uke's elbow. He accomplishes this by extending the fingers of both his hands and bending his right arm inwards. Tori then applies an atemi-waza to uke's right temple [*kasumi*]—striking it with his right *te-gatana* [hand blade] thereby psychologically unbalancing uke, and destroying his concentration—mental kuzushi.

Tori then controls uke by locking his right wrist with Kote-hineri—

clamping uke's right arm under his own left arm as he does so. Tori then uses tai-sabaki—stepping back with his right foot and turning his body to his right, thus further off-balancing uke. Tori finally controls uke with Ude-hishigi-waki-gatame.

Acquiring the Principles

To build a thorough understanding of the riai in Kodokan Goshin-jutsu, its defenses and counterattacks should be practiced deliberately and properly. Greater speed can be progressively introduced as tori improves his avoidance, escape and counter attack skills (Cornish, 1984: 6-7).

For example, recall Ryote-dori. As previously described, tori's reactions to uke grabbing his wrists are multiple—stretch the fingers, withdraw the left leg diagonally to the left, and bend the right arm towards the inside. These actions must occur simultaneously and automatically. Mouri (personal communication, 13 September 2015) recollects being regularly directed by an elderly Kodokan sensei to continually practice the sequence until he could execute it instinctively. Like for all judo, *uchi-komi* [repetition training], where a particular technique is practiced repeatedly to learn the specific kuzushi, tai-sabaki and other technical aspects, has an important role in learning Kodokan Goshin-jutsu. Specifically, uchi-komi helps tori imbed the defenses of Kodokan Goshin-jutsu so that they can be readily applied in a physical emergency.

The role of uke in supporting tori to develop an understanding of the principles is also crucial (Ibid.: 5-6). Cornish explains:

> Uke of course plays an intrinsic part in kata. Some maintain the most important part and we must add his attempted techniques to the knowledge we gain by doing kata. Even though uke's attempts never succeed his techniques must be perfectly feasible and truly attempted. Otherwise both uke's and tori's training will be impaired.
> – Ibid.: 6

Further guidance on acquiring the principles within Kodokan Goshin-jutsu is provided later where its teaching and learning challenges are explicitly considered.

Kodokan Goshin-jutsu as a "Point of Departure"

Real combat always requires the adaptation of previous learning to the genuine attack being experienced. Since the particulars of the actual conflict will never be identical to those in the exercise, it is essential that Kodokan Goshin-jutsu should not be considered in isolation as a prescribed and rigidly fixed success formula, for specific self-defense situations only. Rather, Kodokan Goshin-jutsu should be regarded as a judo exercise that encapsulates a series of self-defense examples that teaches principles that are part of a greater whole, and which through practice helps tori develop and embed self-defense responses that are most likely to result in favorable outcomes. In the engagement, it is uke's actions and tori's own experiences and capabilities that determine which tools to use.

In this way, Kodokan Goshin-jutsu in its standard form was meant to be a "point of departure", with the sequences and techniques therein merely a range of options that could be experimented with during training. Specifically, once the principles of sequential self-defense in the basic form have been mastered, then modifications and variations, consistent with these concepts, can be added and practiced.

Cornish (1984: 30-32) presents examples of many such "alternatives" in his booklet, where he provides solution options to the challenges arising were uke to respond differently than expected. He achieves this by drawing on his extensive personal experience in aikido, and also by substituting other techniques from elsewhere in Kodokan Goshin-jutsu to cope.

The principle in operation here is that one can use judo to survive in *shinken shobu*, with tori having complete freedom of action to respond how he wants, and Kodokan Goshin-jutsu having helped prepare him mentally and physically for the challenge. In this way Kodokan Goshin-jutsu is a valuable part of a broader judo curriculum, and a reminder of, and bridge to, the self-defense aspects of judo that are typically ignored nowadays[58].

TEACHING AND LEARNING KODOKAN GOSHIN-JUTSU

Some of the issues associated with teaching and learning, Kodokan Goshin-jutsu will now be reflected upon. Included in this will be a review of a selection of Kodokan Goshin-jutsu learning resources that are available to support both teachers, and students.

Teaching and Learning Challenges

Like many other aspects of judo, Kodokan Goshin-jutsu only makes sense when one personally has a high degree of judo understanding, technical sophistication and competence. This is usually predicated on one having been expertly taught[59], and for this purpose the annual Kodokan Summer Kata Course is popular with judoka looking to improve their competencies through direct instruction from senior Kodokan teachers. Figure 13 shows judoka practicing the staff attacks from Kodokan Goshin-jutsu's Buki-no-bu during the 2015 Kodokan Summer Kata Course.

As a teaching approach, it is recommended that Kodokan Goshin-jutsu be first placed in its proper context. This should include an explanation of the purpose of the exercise, including the historical background to its development and the intentions of its creators.

Kodokan Goshin-jutsu's defenses against the standard attacks can be taught and learnt next. As a learning approach, grouping the sequences into holistic sets of related actions, rather than considering each one individually, is helpful (Cornish, 1984: 5) as it enables the principles to be introduced. When considering the physical mechanics of the defenses, prominence should also be given to ensuring realism and strong spirit.

Once progress is made in learning Kodokan Goshin-jutsu's mechanics ("the how"), then greater understanding of the *riai* or reasons and principles behind each and every movement ("the why") should be developed. Acquiring this understanding is best achieved through a twin-track process that simultaneously addresses both the fundamental and the specific principles. For example, kuzushi and tai-sabaki skills are fundamental principles to all of judo, whereas self-confidence, situational awareness, escape methods, atemi-waza and their linkages to nage-waza or katame waza in a conflict situation are principles more specific to Kodokan Goshin-jutsu.

Figure 13: The *Tsue-no-baai* [staff attacks] from the Buki-no-bu section of Kodokan Goshin-jutsu being practiced during the 2015 Kodokan Summer Kata Course.

RESOURCES FOR LEARNING KODOKAN GOSHIN-JUTSU

A range of the written and filmed material for teaching and learning Kodokan Goshin-jutsu is now be reviewed. Note that texts by Tomiki (1958),

Kotani (1962), Kotani et al (1968), Kodokan (1976), Cornish (1984), and Hamot et al (1985) all show the original conclusion to haimen-zuke where uke is merely disarmed and not thrown.

1958, Kenji Tomiki: *Kodokan Goshin-jutsu*

Tomiki's 1958 book *Kodokan Goshin-jutsu* (shown earlier in Figure 5) is the first and most important book on the exercise. The 144-page text provides an illustrated explanation of the complete Kodokan Goshin-jutsu—including step-by-step black and white photographs of the attacks and defenses, line drawings of the footwork patterns, and advice on how to execute the wristlocks and various atemi-waza. However, consistent with the informal intent for Kodokan Goshin-jutsu, no emphasis is given to any reiho aspects. Recall in this original text, the final technique, haimen-zuke concludes with tori simply disarming uke by capturing the gun.

The demonstrators are Tomiki himself as tori, and Mr. Sakamoto, a former captain of the Waseda University Judo Club as uke. Regrettably as with many Japanese judo books of that vintage, the paper is delicate and the printed photographs are of poor quality. The text is only available on the used book market, and given its historical significance, the asking price is often high. For these reasons its major usefulness is for reference and research purposes, rather than a practical text for studying Kodokan Goshin-jutsu.

1955 and later 1976 reprint, Kodokan, editors: *Illustrated Kodokan Judo*

The original 1955 edition of this classic text from the Kodokan does not contain Kodokan Goshin-jutsu, as it was still in development. However, the later 1976 reprint does. Chapter XIV (Kodokan, 1976: 209-216) presents a well-illustrated explanation of the exercise's mechanical movements and a succinct summary of its purpose and content:

> The *Kodokan Goshinjutsu* (methods of self-defence) includes, together with the *Kime-no-kata* (forms of self-defence), devices for actual fighting. In this category are included the best and most typical devices against conceivable grappling, choking, striking, thrusting or kicking attacks from the opponent, as well as tricks against various forms of violence—the dagger, the staff and the pistol. When these methods were finally established by the Kodokan in 1956, much consideration was necessitated to make them suitable and up-to-date, and yet distinct from those techniques of the *Kime-no-kata* (forms of self-defence). In these methods, all the tricks of the punching technique, the throwing technique and the seizing technique culminate...
>
> – Ibid.: 209

Despite being small, the black and white photographs serve well as a memory aid, and for an experienced judoka are sufficient for starting to learn the exercise. In the photographs, tori is the late Masao Koyasu, Kodokan 9th dan and uke is thought to be the late Kiyoji Suzuki, Kodokan 9th dan (Kodokan, personal communication, 20 November 2015).

1961, Kodokan: *Judo*

The book *Judo*, which was published in 1961 to mark the centenary of Jigoro Kano's birth, devotes six pages to Kodokan Goshin-jutsu (Kodokan, 1961: 74-79). A summary descriptive paragraph on the exercise is included, and a series of large black and white photographs, used to show five representative techniques from across the entire exercise. The photographs show two sequences drawn from the Oshu-no-bu section and three from the Buki-no-bu section. In the photographs, Tomiki is tori and Oba is uke.

Figure 14: Outtake from the Kodokan Goshin-jutsu pages from the 1961 book *Judo* which was published to mark the centenary of Jigoro Kano's birth. The techniques shown are *maegeri* [front kick] and *nanametsuki* [slanting stab]. Kenji Tomiki is tori [the one demonstrating the technique] and Hideo Oba is uke [the one attacking].

    The two Toshu-no-bu sequences are Ushiro-jime from the Kumitsu-kareta-baai, and maegeri from the Hanareta-baai. The three Buki-no-bu sequences are Naname-tsuki from the Tanto-no-baai, Morote-tsuki from the Tsue-no-baai, and haimen-zuke from the Kenshu-no-baai. Very limited descriptive text on the sequences is provided—see Figure 14 for the mae-geri and Naname-tsuki examples. Recall also that haimen-zuke in this book ends with tori throwing uke with Kote-gaeshi, and that this is the first example of this conclusion known to the authors (Ibid.: 78).

The book is not really a learning resource for Kodokan Goshin-jutsu, but is highly desirable for its historical content. It would be a valuable addition to the library of anyone interested in the history of judo.

1968, Sumiyuki Kotani, Yoshimi Osawa & Yuichi Hirose:
Kata of Kodokan Judo & *Kata of Kodokan Judo Revised*

The technical kata books written by Kotani and others in the late 1960s and early 1970s remain the primary reference texts for the serious study of kata. With respect to Kodokan Goshin-jutsu, Kotani et al's, translated, *Kata of Kodokan Judo*, Figure 15, and its near-identical reprint *Kata of Kodokan Judo Revised* were, prior to Cornish (1984), the most technically detailed study texts available in the English language (Kotani et al, 1968: 54-91). It is worthy to note that as well as Kotani, another of these books' co-authors went on to receive the illustrious grade of Kodokan 10th dan, with Yoshimi Osawa (born 1926), Figure 16, being promoted to that level in 2006.

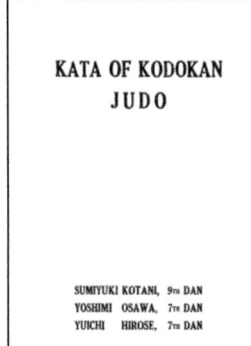

Figure 15 (left): *Kata of Kodokan Judo* by Kotani et al. was published in 1968 and is a detailed text for studying the various Kodokan kata.
Figure 16 (right): Yoshimi Osawa (born 1926)—pictured here in 1958.

Beyond explaining Kodokan Goshin-jutsu's mechanics, the books also describe its important principles, and provide helpful guidelines for practice. They also contain relatively small black and white photographs of the exercise's mechanical movements, as well as footwork patterns for each sequence (Ibid.). In the photographs, Kotani is tori and Yuichi Hirose is uke.

Note that the placement of the weapons shown in these books is the opposite of what is standard today, with the gun, rather than the knife, being closest to uke (Ibid.: 56). This however is most likely a simple mistake, rather than a different historical convention, and in no way detracts from their overall merit.

1971, Sumiyuki Kotani & Tadao Otaki: *Saishin Judo-no-Kata Zen*

The previously mentioned Japanese language book *Saishin Judo-no-Kata Zen* by Kotani and Otaki (1971) is a 324-page text containing seven Kodokan kata. To this day it remains the kata textbook of choice for dedicated Japanese judoka. The book, Figure 17, contains a relatively detailed description of Kodokan Goshin-jutsu, though again only relatively small, black and white photographs (Ibid.: 119-169). Katsuyoshi Takata, a noted Kodokan sensei in his own right, see later, was the photographer.

Figure 17 (left): *Saishin Judo-no-Kata Zen* by Kotani and Otaki was published in 1971 and remains the kata textbook of choice for keen Japanese judoka.
Figure 18 (right): *Kodokan Goshin Jutsu* by John Cornish was published in 1984 and is an indepth English language resource for learning the exercise.

1984, John Cornish: *Go-Shin-Jutsu – Judo Self Defence Kata*

John P. Cornish (born 1929) is a senior British judoka (presently BJA 7th dan) and aikidoka (presently 8th dan). He studied judo from 1952 at the London Budokwai[60] under the celebrated British judoka, author, broadcaster and scholar Trevor (T.P.) Leggett (1914-2000) Kodokan 6th dan. From 1958 to 1964 he practiced both systems in Japan—specifically, judo at the Kodokan as a member of the *Kenshusei* [research student] class, and aikido and the Hombu [Headquarters] dojo. In particular, he studied Kodokan Goshin-jutsu as a direct student of Kenji Tomiki. After his return to the UK, he taught both judo and aikido at the Budokwai until his retirement in 2010.

In the early 1980s Cornish published a booklet entitled *Go-Shin-Jutsu— Judo Self Defence Kata* (Cornish, 1984), Figure 18. Together with Kotani et al's 1968 translated texts, it is the most technically detailed written resource on Kodokan Goshin-jutsu available in the English language. As well as benefiting from large and clear black and white photographs of the exercise's mechanical movements, it presents a complete dissection of each attack and defense sequence—including a valuable explanation of the underlying principles at work, as well as guidelines for "further study".

While clearly effective, the Kodokan Goshin-jutsu shown by Cornish is of its time, and differs in several places from today's accepted standard. As a direct student of Tomiki, it is unsurprising that what Cornish presents is comparable to that in Tomiki's original text (Tomiki, 1958). None of these differences detract from the merit of Cornish's booklet, and it is highly recommended as essential reading for anyone seriously interested in the exercise.

1985, George Parulski: *Black Belt Judo*

In the book *Black Belt Judo* published under the auspices of the now defunct American Society of Classical Judoka, George Parulski Jr. presents a summary description of Kodokan Goshin-jutsu:

> Kodokan Goshin-jutsu: Translated as the 'Kodokan's method of self-defense', this kata was invented in the '50s by a staff of masters at the Kodokan. Their intention was to update the techniques of the Kime-no-kata for modern times. This kata contains methods of throwing, holding, evading kicking, striking and choking. There are defenses against bare hands, staffs, knives and guns.
> – Parulski, 1985: 74

Parulski provides no further specific content on Kodokan Goshin-jutsu. He does however provide detailed instructions on various self-defense techniques—including various atemi-waza (Ibid.: 157-173), and also some self-defense sequences (Ibid.: 174-181). These are interesting in their own right.

1985, Claude Hamot, Guy Pelletier & Claude Urvoy: *Katame no Kata Kodokan Goshin Jutsu*

Hamot, Pelletier and Urvoy's 1985 French-language book *Katame no Kata Kodokan Goshin Jutsu* presents clear black and white photographs with limited accompanying narrative that deals only with the mechanics of Kodokan Goshin-jutsu. The attacks and defense movements shown are like those in Tomiki (1958), Kotani and Otaki (1971) and Cornish (1984). As mentioned earlier, the etiquette involves sitting bowing arrangements.

Note that one of the authors, Guy Pelletier (1921-2011) Kodokan 8th dan, FFJDA 9th dan, was until his death, the world's highest ranking Kodokan-graded judoka of non-Japanese descent. For this reason alone, the book is of historical interest.

1986, Jigoro Kano: *Illustrated Kodokan Judo*

This book, published by Kodansha, and presenting Jigoro Kano as its author, was actually compiled by a Kodokan editorial committee long after the Shihan's death. It is a more recent update of the original 1955 *Kodokan Judo*, and contains descriptions of all formally recognized techniques, and eight judo kata—including Kodokan Goshin-jutsu.

Like in the 1976 expanded reprint of the 1955 standard, the instructional text on Kodokan Goshin-jutsu is concise and focuses on mechanical movements only. Similarly, the black and white photographs, this time with the late Kazuhiko Kawabe, Kodokan 8th dan as tori and Tsuyoshi Sato, Kodokan 8th dan as uke, are small. The book however is a good resource for starting to learn Kodokan Goshin-jutsu, and given its availability in Japanese, English, French and German, probably represents the most popular introductory text.

1987 & 1992, Kodokan:
Kodokan Goshin-jutsu (with K. Takata & T. Sengoku)

Following the conclusion of the review by the Kodokan's Kodokan Goshin-jutsu Research Committee, a new teaching booklet was published (Kodokan, 1987). This booklet aimed to present a unified and standardized Kodokan Goshin-jutsu, and clarified some of the exercise's key points—including the protocol for weapons handling, and the positioning of tori and uke. The booklet was available in both Japanese and English, with the English version being a full, Kodokan-produced, high quality translation of the Japanese original (Kodokan, personal communication, 11 December 2015). In the photographs, Katsuyoshi Takata is tori and Tsueno Sengoku is uke—at the time holders of Kodokan 8th dan and 7th dan respectively. Additionally, and most notably, the conclusion of haimen-zuke in the booklet had tori throwing uke with a Kote-gaeshi, type technique and the photographs for this technique were accompanied, for the first time, by a suitably detailed instructional narrative (Ibid.: 45-46).

Figure 19:

Ude-hishigi-te-gatame [arm crushing hand armlock] from *Hidari-eri-dori* [left-lapel hold] in the *toshi-no-bu* [unarmed attacks] section of Kodokan Goshin-jutsu as shown in the 1987 Kodokan-produced instructional booklet. Katsuyoshi Takata is tori [the one demonstrating the technique] and Tsueno Sengoku is uke [the one attacking].

Both Takata and Sengoku have been important Kodokan teachers of Kodokan Goshin-jutsu, and for this reason, further information on these two senior judoka is now provided.

Katsuyoshi Takata (1921-2000), Figure 20, was a dynamic and inspirational Kodokan teacher and a prominent kata expert in the period following the retirement[61] of Kotani. Takata, like his mentor Kotani, was known to focus extensively on Kodokan Goshin-jutsu's principles—emphasizing in particular its aiki-jujutsu heritage in his search for maximum effectiveness.

Takata was also nicknamed "Mr. Hanegoshi" due to his well-known mastery of the technique[62] [*hanegoshi* = spring hip throw], and authored a bilingual (Spanish and English) book describing thirteen different methods of executing the throw (Takata, 1961). Takata achieved the rank of Kodokan 8th dan during his lifetime, and on his death in 2000 was posthumously promoted to Kodokan 9th dan (Oltremari, n.d.).

Figure 20 (left): Katsuyoshi Takata (1921-2000).
Figure 21 (right): Tsueno Sengoku (born 1945).

Tsueno Sengoku (born 1945) presently Kodokan 8th dan, Figure 21, has been a Kodokan teacher and member of its core kata staff. Additionally, he has been a senior judo instructor at the *Keishicho* [Tokyo Metropolitan Police Department] and is also highly experienced in *taiho-jutsu* [arresting art]—a well-established system for law enforcement professionals, synthesized from koryu, *gendai budo* [modern martial ways][63] and Western boxing. As well as being a dedicated uke to Takata, Sengoku is probably best known, along with Tadashi Sato presently Kodokan 8th dan, as a demonstrator in Daigo's definitive book on nage-waza—*Kodokan Judo: Throwing Techniques* (Daigo, 2005). Currently Sengoku resides in Indonesia where a large modern judo center, the Sengoku International Judo Hall, has been built in Bali, and named after him.

1998, Pedro Dabauza:
Kata Judo-Jujitsu: Formas Antiguas y Modernas de Defensa Personal

Pedro Rodríguez Dabauza (born 1949) is a Spanish budoka who holds high-dan rank in both judo—presently DNBK 8th dan, RFEJYDA[64] 8th dan, and non-koryu jujutsu. He is a multi-published author, a producer of several budo instructional films and a regular teacher and participant at international budo seminars.

Kata Judo-Jujitsu: Formas Antiguas y Modernas de Defensa Personal [*Judo-Jujitsu Kata: Old and Modern Forms of Self Defence*] is a Spanish-language text that, as its title suggests, covers both the old, Kime-no-kata, and modern, Kodokan Goshin-jutsu, self-defense forms. Also included is a concise overview on Kano's contribution to judo as well, as several souvenir photographs of the author with many noted Kodokan teachers (Dabauza, 1998: 129-155).

The Kodokan Goshin-jutsu section (Ibid., 17-69) contains true, still black and white photographs of the exercise, with Dabauza himself, then a 6th dan, as tori, and Jorge Cuevas, then a 5th dan, as uke. Succinct instructive text for all of the sequences is provided, as well as a summary of their main principles.

2003, Kisaburo Watanabe: *Essential Judo Katas*

Kisaburo Watanabe (born 1936) Kodokan 8th dan is a past Asian Games judo champion, and was resident coach at the London Budokwai from 1962 to 1966. To coincide with the 1993 kata championships, organized by the now-defunct World Masters Judo Association[65] (WMJA), he produced a 214 page book with instructions for five Kodokan kata. Kodokan Goshin-jutsu is the fifth one described therein (Watanabe, 2003: 165-213).

The book was printed in limited numbers and was not openly for sale. The book contains black line drawings and simple, limited instructions. For these reasons it represents a helpful quick-reference guide for use on the tatami, rather than a resource for serious learning.

2004 & 2015, Kodokan:
Kodokan Goshin-jutsu (with K. Onozawa & K. Komata)

Between 2004 and 2008 the Kodokan published a series of kata instructional booklets for use in conjunction with the appropriate Kodokan teaching film. Six booklets were produced, covering seven Kodokan kata, with Itsutsu-no-kata and Koshiki-no-kata featuring in the same booklet. Originally available in Japanese only, the booklets contained a limited narrative but were well illustrated with black and white photographs. These however, were non-crisp snapshots taken from the video title.

The Kodokan Goshin-jutsu booklet, Figure 22, was published in 2004 and replaced the earlier volume featuring Takata and Sengoku. Being derived from the film, the new booklet (Kodokan, 2004) also had Onozawa as tori and Komata as uke. Presently, both Onozawa and Komata hold the rank of Kodokan 8th dan.

In 2015 the Kodokan released five of the kata booklets in the English language—including Kodokan Goshin-jutsu (Kodokan, 2015), Figure 23. These were based on an official translation of the 2004-2008 booklets, with significantly expanded contents provided by the translator, Lance Gatling, working with a number of senior Kodokan instructors. Additional, purpose-shot, black and white photographs were introduced throughout, as well as more details of the various kata's mechanical movements.

Figure 22: The Kodokan's study booklet for Kodokan Goshin-jutsu—produced in 2004, originally in Japanese only.

Figure 23: The Kodokan's expanded English language study booklet for Kodokan Goshin-jutsu released in 2015.

2005, Masao Takahashi (& Family): *Mastering Judo*

The book *Mastering Judo* presents a broad based overview of judo's philosophy, history, techniques, tactics, and training methods. The authors—Masao Takahashi and family—(wife, June and children Allyn, Phil, Ray, and Tina) all hold high dan rank in judo, and between them have over 200 years of judo experience. The principal author and family patriarch, Masao Takahashi presently holds the rank of Judo Canada 8th dan.

The book presents a tabulated description of the mechanics of Kodokan Goshin-jutsu, with separate summary descriptions of the roles of uke and tori for each attack and defense sequence (Takahashi, 2005: 55-56). Takahashi provides no illustrations of Kodokan Goshin-jutsu itself, however later, detailed well illustrated instructional material on various judo self-defense techniques (Ibid.: 169-194) is provided.

2007, Tadao Inogai & Roland Habersetzer: *Judo Kata—Les Formes Classiques du Kodokan*

Tadao Inogai (1908-1978) Kodokan 8th dan in conjunction with the French budoka Roland Habersetzer (born 1942), has several French language judo books to his name. The text, *Judo Kata–Les Formes Classiques du Kodokan* [*Judo Kata–Kodokan Classic Forms*] which has become an essential source for serious French judoka, presents eight Kodokan kata through clear, two-color, line drawings and reasonably detailed instructions. Despite the erroneous use of the name Goshin-jutsu-no-kata throughout (Inogai and Habersetzer, 2007: 161-210), the book does represent a very helpful, quick-reference, guide that enables the exercise's mechanical movements to be readily learnt.

2009, Shu Taira: *La Essencia del Judo*

La Essencia del Judo [*The Essence of Judo*], Figure 24, is an ambitious and meticulously prepared study of judo from a technical, historical and philosophical perspective, due to Shu Taira (born 1942), presently RFEJYDA 9th dan. Shu Taira has resided in Spain since 1967, and is the son of Tsuson Taira (1901-1988), himself a Kodokan 8th dan.

La Essencia del Judo was first published, in two (sold together) volumes, in 2009, and reprinted in 2015. The first volume is about the history of judo, nage-waza and katame waza, while the second focuses on kata and also contains the appendices. The section on Kodokan Goshin-jutsu (Taira, 2009: 253-314) contains a good explanation of the exercise's history, principles and mechanics, and is lavishly illustrated with high quality photographs, with Taira himself as tori, and an unknown uke. The book is very desirable, relatively expensive and available in Spanish only. Nevertheless, it is highly recommended to all serious judoka.

Post 2009, FFJDA: *Kodokan Goshinjitsu*

The "Guide du judoka" series of booklets and accompanying DVDs created by the FFJDA are training resources designed for both judo teachers and students to discover, or rediscover, the technical subtleties of kata practice. Produced in the French language, the materials are approved by the FFJDA's National Technical Directorate and the High Grades Commission. The third booklet and DVD in the series feature Kodokan Goshin-jutsu and are undated—however, they are known to have been produced sometime after 2009, as the preceding booklet and DVD on Katame-no-kata, the second in the series, is dated for then.

The booklet and DVD themselves are entitled *Kodokan Goshinjitsu*, Figure 25, which is a common error made by those unfamiliar with the nuances of transliteration from Japanese writing systems to the Roman alphabet.

Involved in the preparation of the material were FFJDA high grades Michel Algisi, Michel Casse, Michèle Lionnet, Patrice Berthoux and André Boutin along with French international kata competitors Frédéric Guillaume and Sevestre Esteve.

As would be expected from the FFJDA, the booklet itself is well produced. Each attack and defense series is illustrated with three photographs which are stills from the DVD. The narrative for each sequence is structured into three sections—general principles, how to perform the series and overall advice.

Figure 24 (left): *La Esencia del Judo* by Shu Taira was published in 2009 and is a Spanish-language in-depth study of judo from a technical, historical and philosophical perspective

Figure 25 (center): *Kodokan Goshinjitsu* (sic.) produced by the FFJDA is a well produced French-language guide for learning the exercise.

Figure 26 (right): *Kodokan Goshin Jutsu* by Blonk et al was published in 2010 and is a good Dutch-language guide for learning the exercise.

2010, Mas Blonk, Richard de Bijl & Ferry van Dijk:
Kodokan Goshin Jutsu

In *Kodokan Goshin-jutsu*, Figure 26, the fifth book of their series on the Kodokan kata, Mas Blonk (born 1944) and Richard de Bijl (born 1952), supported by Ferry van Dijk (born 1933), address the issue that the exercise is barely described in the Dutch judo literature. The authors are kodansha of the JBN[66], with Blonk and de Bijl presently holding the rank of JBN 8th dan and van Dijk, JBN 7th dan.

It is correctly acknowledged in the book that Kodokan Goshin-jutsu is not formally a kata, and that although the order of the sequences is defined, tori has considerable freedom in how he performs the defenses. In this way the authors are faithfully describing the spirit originally intended for Kodokan Goshin-jutsu, though they do suggest a normalized set of attacks and defenses. The book contains clear descriptions of the sequences and is well illustrated with insightful photographs. In this way it is an important guide for the proper practice of Kodokan Goshin-jutsu.

FILMED INSTRUCTIONAL MATERIALS FOR *KODOKAN GOSHIN-JUTSU*

A selection of recommended filmed materials on Kodokan Goshin-jutsu are now reviewed.

1998 & 2009, Kodokan:
Kodokan Judo Kata Series–Kodokan Goshin-jutsu

In January 1998 the Kodokan produced on VHS tape a 45-minute long *Kodokan Goshin-jutsu* instructional film (Kodokan, 1998). Recall that this film, with Onozawa and Komata, forms the basis of the subsequent Kodokan teaching booklets (Kodokan, 2004; 2015). As well as presenting a demonstration of the complete exercise, the film provided commentary on the correct forms of each technique including a precise explanation of the correct mechanical movements.

The film was re-edited in September 2009 and released on DVD (Kodokan, 2009). A welcome addition was the inclusion of some excerpts from Tomiki and Otaki's original 1956 demonstration.

2006, Kano Society: *Kodokan Goshin-jutsu*

The Kano Society was founded in 2000 by a group of senior British judoka concerned that judo was no longer being taught or practiced according to the principles espoused by Kano. Their goal was to promote the style of judo that was once prevalent.

In support of this purpose the Society has been compiling a number of DVDs—including a two-part Kodokan Goshin-jutsu teaching film, featuring John Cornish teaching (in October 2005) at the now closed "Sleeping Storm Aikido" dojo in Epsom, UK. The discs are separately sold with "Part 1—Toshu (against an unarmed attack)", and "Part 2—Buki (against an armed attack)" (Kano Society, 2006). The Kodokan Goshin-jutsu shown on the DVDs is identical to that presented in Cornish's booklet (Cornish, 1984). The earlier comments on that work also apply here.

As already highlighted, Cornish's teaching is rooted in his own judo background and he regards all kata as a training resource. The DVDs do not present a complete ceremonial performance of Kodokan Goshin-jutsu and are caveated:

This series of instructional videos are intended as an aid to study of the Kata (and not as a formal 'demonstration').

– Ibid.

Cornish's commitment to Kodokan Goshin-jutsu is clear from the film, and even at an advanced age his enthusiasm for the exercise is undiminished. While the vital kuzushi is not emphasized in all the demonstrations, the wrist techniques are clearly strong and effective[67]. The teaching style throughout the films is relaxed and genial, and as Cornish retired from all teaching in 201 these films represent the best opportunity to benefit from the experience of someone who learnt Kodokan Goshin-jutsu at source—that is directly from its creators in its formative years.

INTERNET SOURCES

Nowadays, Kodokan Goshin-jutsu demonstrations and teaching materials are freely viewable on videosharing websites such as *YouTube* and *Vimeo*. These include film recordings made at the Kodokan Summer Kata Course and also at various kata championships—see later. Some archive film footage of great teachers such as Tomiki, Kotani and Takata is also available. Such material is easily found using any search engine and will not be specifically referenced here. Finally, while most of the web-based material really only helps with Kodokan Goshin-jutsu's mechanics, and is not of benchmark standard, it can still be helpful and inspiring.

PERFORMING AND COMPETING IN KODOKAN GOSHIN-JUTSU

Performance Aspects

As explained earlier, kata were designed as a learning resource and the original intent for kata practice was that judoka would select a few sequences from a listed kata, say and simply study them as a core part of training. Therefore, it was never intended that ceremonial performances of complete kata would be the most common form of practice, and despite formal renditions of whole kata being today's norm, such presentations were initially only intended to be part of a judo *enbu* [ceremonial demonstration] to an audience.

In a personal communication, Cornish reinforces this point, and explains how complete performances with high degrees of finesse are unnecessary.

In my years as a British National Coach for kata I have, and still do, try to explain that the demonstration of kata is not important, it is the training, and what [principles] you learn from the training, that counts. For so much of judo, kata is the only way that training in safety can be carried out.

– J.P. Cornish, personal communication, 3 June 2000

The above point is particularly true for Kodokan Goshin-jutsu, which is the application of a pedagogical system (judo) to self-defense. As has been explained, the primary goal, and mindset, for practice should not be one of "perfecting" the mechanical movements of the complete performance sequence, but rather one of developing an understanding of the principles of judo self-defense. Kotani et al also counsel:

… judo players… are apt to practice only the forms of Goshinjitsu [sic.] and forget acquiring the essentials of Goshinjitsu [sic.]…"
– Kotani et al, 1968: 57

The Impact of Kata Competitions

No contemporary article on kata in judo would be complete without considering the impact being made by kata competitions, which have markedly grown in popularity in recent years (Jones and Hanon, 2010).

One consequence of the Kodokan formally treating Kodokan Goshin-jutsu as a proper kata is that it now features in most organized kata competitions. Interestingly however, there was no Kodokan Goshin-jutsu category in the first, and so far only, Kodokan Judo Kata International Tournament. This event was organized jointly by the Kodokan and the All Japan Judo Federation, and held in Tokyo in October 2007 (Gatling, 2008).

Figure 27: Tomoo Hamana as tori and Masayoshi Yamazaki as uke, winning the Kodokan Goshin-jutsu category at the 2011 International Judo Federation (IJF) World Judo Kata Championships held in Frankfurt, Germany. The technique shown in the photograph is *kote-gaeshi* [wrist reversal] from *naname-tsuki* [slanting stab].

The Positives and Negatives

It is evident that the introduction of kata-specific tournaments has broadened the appeal of kata by providing judoka with new sources of motivation for its study. These include the prospect of winning a medal, or of becoming an international-level competitor via the alternative pathway that "competitive kata" provides.

As a direct consequence of kata championships, there are presently more judoka aware of, and practicing kata, than at any time in the recent past. However, in the long-term, the drift of kata into the "realm of sport", especially under the rules of the IJF with a scoring system[68] that focuses on mistakes and points deductions (for deviations from a supposed reference standard) could do more harm than good. Of particular concern is the idea that there exists an ideal standard kata, as such thinking contradicts the principle of *shu-ha-ri* [protect-break-separate][69]—the traditional route of progressing from basic knowledge to mastery in Japan[70]. Specifically, the current approach to judging kata is overly weighted on the *shu* component, with minimal scope in the scoring system to accommodate the *ha* or the *ri* elements (Jones and Hanon, 2010).

In the case of Kodokan Goshin-jutsu, the emphasis on the principles within has diminished[71], and that on mechanical movements increased. For this reason, the Kodokan Goshin-jutsu performances seen in contemporary kata tournaments are sometimes over-stylized self-parodies with unrealistic techniques, and markedly different from Tomiki and Otaki's first demonstration (Kodokan, 2009; Sharp, 2013) which was full of realism, spirit and effective technique.

Authors' Comments

Kata were not created to be "judged" or to be studied as an exercise in "how to perform a complete ceremonial kata demonstration"—rather they were developed as a living and breathing educational tool to support the correct learning and practice of judo principles (Jones and Hanon, 2010). However, for better or worse, competitive kata is here to stay, and with this the risk of future generations of judoka believing this significant misrepresentation of kata is the norm. This is exemplified by the particularly uninformed definition of kata from USA Judo[72]:

> Kata is a forms-based judo discipline in which two athletes perform a set routine of judo techniques which are then scored by a panel of judges.
> – Jomantas: 2009

Given the original intent for kata, participation in competitive kata should ideally be viewed as an opportunity to validate one's training, improve one's judo under highly stressful circumstances and obtain feedback for future improvement. However, this requires that the judges doing the critiquing have themselves an in-depth knowledge of kata that goes beyond the capability to notice IJF-specified mistakes.

CREDIBILITY OF KODOKAN GOSHIN-JUTSU FOR SELF-DEFENSE

Much in the way that many think Nage-no-kata and Katame-no-kata are irrelevant to modern sports competitive judo, there are those who believe that Kodokan Goshin-jutsu is neither a complete, nor an effective system of self-defense (Michael J. Hanon, personal communication, 24 November 2013). Often, but not always, this unjust criticism comes from those persons whose learning has been limited to Kodokan Goshin-jutsu's performance aspects[73] and who have not studied and explored its core principles, or how they translate to self-defense (C. De Crée, personal communication, 25 November 2013). Since Kodokan Goshin-jutsu is nowadays treated as a kata, the remark of Fraguas (2001) is particularly relevant:

> Unfortunately, 95 percent of the people don't understand kata —only the outside movements which are irrelevant without understanding.
> – Fraguas, 2001: 283

The principal points of criticism for Kodokan Goshin-jutsu are whether or not it provides one with the tools for effectively dealing with knife and pistol attacks. To a degree this is understandable, but again has at its source an over-emphasis on mechanical movements, and an under-appreciation of principles. To address this issue, further explanation of the defenses against knife and pistol attacks will now be presented. This will draw on Cornish (1984: 22-24; 27-33) and Wolfgang Dax-Romswinkel (personal communication, 27 November 2013).

Knife Attacks

The knife attacks in Kodokan Goshin-jutsu include a sudden draw and thrust, a lunge, and a slanting slash from above. They encompass what would be the most common types of knife attack, and therefore represent a sufficiently complete set of generic situations for developing self-defense concepts and principles.

Defenses against a determined attacker armed with a knife are difficult and dangerous to execute, so tori has to study the Tanto-no-baai sequences very deeply. The essential principles in the defenses are tai-sabaki, to evade the attack and remain in a relatively safe position, and kuzushi to distract and disturb uke's equilibrium. These two aspects cannot be over-emphasized for knife defenses, and failure to perform them perfectly in a "real situation" could well result in tori's death. Above all else, the emphasis in their practice has to be on realism and effectiveness.

Consider, for example, the first knife-defense—Tsukkake, which arguably is the most difficult defense in all of Kodokan Goshin-jutsu. In this defense, tori foils uke's attack in the preparatory stage[74], with the intended attack being first countered with tai-sabaki in such a way as to shatter it. It is the errors in uke's own actions that provide an opportunity for tori to counter-attack and prevail.

Uke turns to his right to draw the knife from the (virtual) sheath inside his judo jacket, and as a result his left shoulder turns forward and inward. Uke's knife-holding (right) arm is (back) out of tori's reach, and so tori has no option but to attack the other (forward, left) arm. Tori steps forward to take up a position to uke's left rear, so as to be reasonably safe should his counter-attack fail. Tori instantly uses atemi-waza by applying a blinding strike [*metsubushi*] to uke's eyes with the outstretched fingers of his left hand. Tori then immediately grasps uke's left wrist and twists it up, while controlling uke's left elbow, pushing it towards his ear, and off balancing him—kuzushi. Then, as uke reacts and attempts to regain his balance, tori's right hand applies pressure onto the raised elbow and pulls uke diagonally forwards and down to the ground, to uke's left, with *hiki-otoshi* [drawing drop].

Even though the knife in uke's right hand remains free, uke does not have the opportunity to use it due to the blinding metsubushi, and the movement and distance that tori maintains from him. Tori then controls uke on the ground through with *ude-hishigi-te-gatame* [arm crushing hand armlock].

Gun Attacks

In his original book on Kodokan Goshin-jutsu, Tomiki seems to regard the Kenshu-no-baai gun defenses as something of an "adventure". This is in the sense that most judoka learning the exercise may not appreciate that the gun defenses are mainly built on the effective use of mental functions, more so than the mechanical movements. Tomiki writes:

> Needless to say, is totally absurd to compare, or compete, the speed of bodily action against that of a bullet. But there can be various mental states in the mind of a gunman until he actually pulls the trigger. In the process of an attack, one should be able to take advantage of the slightest lack in an attacker's concentration. On the whole, there is no difference in the attitude of a person facing a weapon, be it a gun or something else,

but in case of a gun, a scientific weapon, special caution is in order. Further on, Professor Kudo 9th dan at the Police Academy suggested three points of great importance in dealing with a similar situation:

1. Never make any move until a gunman comes within reach of your hands. While watching carefully his moves, stay alert, but very calm, so as not to cause any agitation.
2. Any defense action should start by first pushing the gun away, use your hands and hips but not your legs.
3. Once such action is initiated, it has to be decisive as you do it at the risk of your life.

– Tomiki, 1958

Additionally, one of the high-ranking judoka at the *Keishicho* [Tokyo Metropolitan Police Department] supervised an empirical study that tested the practicality of executing the three Kenshu-no-bai defenses. In the experiments, the participants were wearing appropriate safety clothing and were using pistols that fired plastic bullets. The study concluded that some 80% of the time, tori was shot while attempting the techniques, and the concluding words regarding the practical application of the defenses was "Very difficult" (O. Mouri, personal communication, 6 April 2015).

It is beyond the scope of this chapter to second-guess such research, but the authors assume it very difficult to duplicate the gun attack situations envisioned in Kodokan Goshin-jutsu for training purposes—an untrained, unsuspecting, naive gunman[75] that has his attention diverted. In any instance, the conclusion reported above should be fully recognized, and the pistol defenses viewed for use only *in extremis*. Indeed, most military and law enforcement professionals with combatives[76] and defensive tactics experience, would not claim to have seen a sufficiently reliable technique for disarming a gunman, that they would recommend for use, unless they observed indicators that lead them to believe they were about to be shot.

Authors' Comments

Kodokan Goshin-jutsu makes a valuable contribution to judo, and none of the issues discussed in this section render it worthless. Indeed, the major criticism of its limited efficacy against guns would apply to all other elements in the entire judo syllabus.

Whether a technique works in "real life" depends on the skill level of the people involved—both attacker and defender. However, in self-defense situations, skill is not the only factor, and recall from earlier, that the ability to physically and emotionally cope with real life conflict and stress, is paramount.

The authors' recommendations to those who believe that an exercise developed by the greatest Kodokan sensei of the time, is fundamentally flawed and futile, is to revisit its learning under a knowledgeable and experienced teacher, focus on principles not mechanics, and then after many years of serious study, reexamine their views.

Concluding Remarks

In the context of judo principles for self-defense, establishing Kodokan Goshin-jutsu was entirely appropriate, since at that time, the only formal exercise for both men and women to study how to attack and defend was the archaic, but still valuable Kime-no-kata.

Knives, staffs and pistols still regularly feature in violent crime today, as do other cutting instruments and firearms. However, nowadays assailants also use new weapons originally developed for law-enforcement, or self-defense purposes, such as electroshock devices or Tasers, CS gas, mace, and pepper sprays. While Kodokan Goshin-jutsu is often referred to as being a "modern self-defense kata", the period for it actually being "modern" was over half a century ago. As Savage (2010; 2013; 2016) points out, critics might argue that Kodokan Goshin-jutsu is as obsolete today as Kime-no-kata was thought to be in the 1950s.

While judo is limited to what it can achieve in terms of defense against any of the aforementioned weapons, this is not a valid reason for discarding Kodokan Goshin-jutsu. The authors firmly believe that Kodokan Goshin-jutsu is fully deserving of its place in contemporary judo—not as a ceremonial performance exercise, or even a method of self-defense, but as a living textbook (Finn, 1991) to practice self-defense principles, and a framework to build and derive additional defenses.

Acknowledgements

The authors would like to register their gratitude to Shinro Fujita, Rie Kurashina and Keiko Otsuki of the International Department of the Kodokan Judo Institute for providing assistance and valuable information whenever requested. Additionally, Figures 11-14, 16 and 19 are reproduced with the permission of the Kodokan Judo Institute, a public interest incorporated foundation. Recall that Figures 1 and 2 are from the personal collection of one of the authors (WLG), whereas Figure 4 was kindly provided by Fumiaki Shishida, Professor of the Intellectual History of the Japanese Martial Arts at

Waseda University, and a direct student of Kenji Tomiki. Figures 9a to 10c and that above the Abstract were made available by professional photographer and judoka, Bob Willingham, and professional photographer and judoka David Finch kindly provided Figure 27. The authors are also indebted to Osamu Mouri for sharing his knowledge of and personal insights into Kodokan Goshin-jutsu—a contribution that significantly enriched the quality of this article. Finally, one of the authors (LCJ) would like to dedicate this work to his own Kodokan Goshin-jutsu teacher—Robert (Bob) Thomas, IJF 8th dan—who inspired in him a deep and abiding interest in the exercise. Any and all errors are our own.

Authors' Note

Japanese names in this chapter are presented given name first and family name second—instead of traditional Japanese usage that places the family name first.

Footnotes

[1] The Kodokan (in full, the Kodokan Judo Institute) is the headquarters of the worldwide judo community. Literally, *ko* means "to lecture" or "to spread information," *do* means "the way," and *kan* is "a public building or hall," together translating roughly as "a place for the study or promotion of the way." The original Kodokan was founded in 1882 at the Eishoji Temple in the Higashi Ueno area of Taito-ku, Tokyo. Today, the Kodokan Judo Institute it is located in a modern eight-story building in Bunkyo-ku, Tokyo.

[2] Since in judo the term "shihan" is used exclusively for Kano, it could be translated as "master".

[3] *Koryu* is a general term for Japanese schools of martial arts that were primarily created by, and for, the warrior class of Japan's feudal period.

[4] Toshiro Daigo (born 1926) was for many years the Chief Instructor at the Kodokan. He was promoted to the rare rank of Kodokan 10th dan in 2006, and is arguably the world's foremost kata expert.

[5] The only formal grouping of kata used by the Kodokan is the collective consideration of Nage-no-kata and Katame-no-kata as *Randori-no-kata* [Forms of Free Exercise]. However, other authors have produced additional groupings for illustrative purposes—notably Kotani, Osawa and Hirose, (1968: 1) and Otaki and Draeger (1983: 32-33). These groupings are Combat, Physical Education, and Theory. Jones and Hanon (2010) provide Japanese terms for these groupings—respectively, Shobu-no-kata, Rentai-no-kata and Ri-no-kata.

[6] Joshi Goshin-ho was developed during the last days of the Second World War (WWII) (1939-1945), when inter alia there was great concern that Japanese women could be physically attacked by invaders. Its creation was

ordered by retired Imperial Japanese Navy Admiral Jiro Nango (1876-1951), a nephew of Kano-shihan, and the second Kodokan Kancho [Head] from 1939 to 1946 (De Crée and Jones, 2011). Careful study of Joshi Goshin-ho reveals that it is tailored towards women in the days when they were mostly clad in kimono, and while judo principles are intermittently applied, the exercise is more founded on a number of specific tricks.

7   In the context of kata, the term *riai* refers to executing the kata in proper accordance with its principles and theory (Dax-Romswinkel, 2015: 44).

8   Dr. Steven Cunningham is a mathematician, economist and former Technical Director of the USJA.

9   USJA = United States Judo Association—one national association for judo in the United States of America.

10 Nango did not personally devise Joshi Goshin-ho—he merely ordered its creation (De Crée and Jones, 2011).

11 Recall that these two exercises are Sei-ryoku Zen'yo Kokumin Taiiku and Joshi Goshin-ho.

12 Sydney (Syd) R. Hoare (born 1939) is a former Chief Instructor of the London Budokwai [sic.] and the London Judo Society, a 1964 Tokyo Olympian and a former Chairman of the BJA. Hoare spent four years training in Japan, is fluent in Japanese, and inter alia is a multi-published author.

13 BJA = British Judo Association (BJA)—the National Governing Body (NGB) for judo in the United Kingdom (UK).

14 Minoru Mochizuki (1907-2003) Kodokan 8th dan was a direct student of both Jigoro Kano and Morihei Ueshiba. He founded the composite system Yoseikan Budo [*Yoseikan* = "Place where the Truth is Taught" or "Place for Practicing what is Right"] and first taught it at his dojo [place of the way – formal training place] in Shizuoka in 1931. Mochizuki held kodansha [high dan] rank in many different budo styles.

15 Aiki-jujutsu was the first (short) term used to describe the jujutsu style more formally known as Daito-ryu Aiki-jujutsu [The Great Eastern School of the Martial Art of Unifying Spirit] (Shishida, 2011).

16 Shinken shobu denotes a real fight to the death, or to a true submission.

17 Tai-sabaki is a general term for movements to shift the position of one's body and change direction in the process of reacting to an opponent's technique and setting up and applying techniques of one's own (Kawamura and Daigo, 2000).

18 The Meiji period extended from 8 September 1868 to 30 July 1912. During this period major socio-political change took place in Japan—with society moving from being isolated and feudal to its modern form.

19 The Edo (or Tokugawa) period is a Japanese era between 1603 and 1868,

when society was under the rule of the Tokugawa bakufu [shogunate] and 300 regional Daimyo [feudal lords]. The period was characterized by economic growth, strict social order, isolationist foreign policies, and popular enjoyment of arts and culture.

20 Samurai were forbidden from entering a daimyo's house, or to be in the presence of the Shogun or the Emperor, while carrying a katana.

21 Note that some who have trained to a very high level in Kime no-kata are known to practice with live blades. This introduces absolute realism into training, and advances the learning and understanding of the kata.

22 During controlled practice, tori and uke are the individuals that apply, and receive, a technique, respectively. In Kimeno-kata and Kodokan Goshin-jutsu, uke makes the initial attack, and tori demonstrates the defensive technique.

23 Also known as Yoshiaki Yamashita.

24 Yamashita was posthumously promoted to 10th dan by Kano on 26 October 1935. However, Kano dated his promotion certificate for two days earlier —thereby making it appear as a substantive promotion.

25 The idea to "modernize" Kime-no-kata had existed since the 1920s, when Jigoro Kano and Kodokan members started to practice *bojutsu* [staff technique] at the Kodokan (Shishida, 2011).

26 Three variations of Nagaoka's given name are often seen—Hidekazu Nagaoka, Shuichi Nagaoka and Hideichi Nagaoka. The correct given name was finally identified via the US National Archives and Records Administration, and the US Immigration Passenger Arrival Records, since when Nagaoka visited Seattle in 1934 he personally signed his entry in romaji as "Nagaoka Hideichi".

27 The influence of Nagaoka might be questioned as being minimal, since he died in November 1952. However, with his koryu background and periods teaching at the Dai Nippon Butokukai and the Busen (its martial arts specialist school) he was an influential figure in Kime-no-kata. By dint of this, it could be considered that he had an impact on the practical combat training of many committee members.

28 Torite is a type of self-defense containing technique for restraining, or escaping from, an attacker.

29 Kudo wrote separate master-volumes on the throwing and grappling techniques of judo under the collective title "Dynamic Judo" (Kudo, 1967; 1967a).

30 Otaki, along with the notable US budoka Donn Draeger (1922-1982) wrote "Judo Formal Techniques" (Otaki and Draeger, 1983) which is to this day the most comprehensive manual on Randori-no-kata.

31 Waseda University is a private university mainly located in Shinjuku,

Tokyo.

32 Towards the end of his life, Kano became increasingly aware of certain failings of judo—not necessarily because of its own flaws, but because the way it was being practiced was increasingly deviating from his original ideas, and also the technical challenges of dealing with assailants using Western boxing techniques attacking from beyond reach. He tried to remedy this by conceding that judo might benefit from an infusion of techniques from koryu jujutsu and even Western boxing. However, this effort apparently never formalized and waned after his death—due to the dislocation caused by WWII, the leadership of Nango, and the subsequent outlawing of martial arts training in public facilities under the Allied occupation of Japan. It was emphasizing judo as a sport that facilitated its eventual return to public facilities.

33 There is no authoritative single list, but a number of different lists with significant overlap.

34 The term *aiki-budo* [the martial way of unifying spirit] began to be used by Ueshiba's pupils (instead of *aiki-jujutsu*) around 1933. In 1942 aiki-budo was renamed aikido—the name still used today (Shishida, 2011).

35 Tomiki was awarded the first 8th dan of aiki-budo by Ueshiba in 1940.

36 For example, there are instances of uke attacking, and tori either failing to grasp him at the first attempt, or else uke breaking free, and tori having to grasp him again.

37 Harold (Hal) E. Sharp (born 1927) is a senior American judoka, and presently a USJA 9th dan. He is Japanese-trained, the author of several popular judo books and also the editor of several judo films of historical interest.

38 *Bujutsu* may be defined as "…combative systems designed by and for warriors to promote self-protection and group solidarity…" (Draeger, 1973: 19).

39 *Budo* may be defined as "…spiritual systems, not necessarily designed by warriors, or for warriors, for the self-protection of the individual…" (Ibid.: 19).

40 Fujoshi-yo-Goshin-no-kata was at one time a suggested name for Joshi Goshin-ho (De Crée and Jones, 2011).

41 FFJDA = Fédération Française de Judo, (Jujitsu, Kendo, Aikido) et Disciplines Associées = French Federation of Judo, (Jujitsu, Kendo, Aikido) and Associated Disciplines—the NGB for judo in France.

42 Kawaishi was posthumously promoted to 10th dan by the FFJDA—the first promotion to this rank by a Western judo NGB (De Crée, 2015).

43 The English language book is a translation by the British journalist, author and judoka Ernest (E.J.) Harrison of the original 1955 French-

language text "Les Katas Complets de Judo" by Kawaishi and Jean Gailhat.

44 The summary of Chapter X wrongly states that Kodokan Goshin-jutsu was established in 1958. Recall that 1958 was the year of publication of Tomiki's original book on Kodokan Goshin-jutsu, and that the exercise itself was established two years earlier in 1956.

45 Although Jigoro Kano is presented as the author of this book—it is in fact a compilation by the Kodokan Judo Institute that dates from long after the founder's death.

46 John P. Cornish is a senior British judoka, BJA 7th dan, and *aikidoka* [a person who practices aikido], 8th dan. He is Japanese-trained and was a direct student of Kenji Tomiki—see later.

47 For clarity, *reigi* is the concept of etiquette and *reiho* is its physical manifestation.

48 During this interim period a few countries, such as France, continued mainly with sitting bowing arrangements—see Hamot, Pelletier and Urvoy (1985).

49 This is excepting of all of the idori section and all of the katana attacks.

50 Ju-no-kata includes a number of attacks and defenses that show the efficient redirection of force and movement. They are not "fighting techniques" in the conventional sense, and there is no notion of literally using them in combat.

51 *Maai* is a complex concept that goes beyond the mere physical distance between the combatants. It is an integration of that distance, with timing, speed, distance, angles, coordination and rhythm of attack.

52 *Mushin* is a mental state into which very highly trained budoka are said to enter during combat. The term is shortened from mushin no shin, a Zen expression meaning "mind of no mind", i.e. a mind not fixed or occupied by thought or emotion, and thus open to everything.

53 *Zanshin* is a state of awareness that continues even after throwing your opponent, maintained to allow further action and response should he continue with a counterattack.

54 In judo, atemi-waza are most often used for the purposes of kuzushi. This contrasts with their use in *karate-do* [empty hand way] where they are an objective in their own right.

55 This is with the exception of one fist attack—Tsukkake and one sword attack—*kirioroshi* [downward cut], both in the tachiai section.

56 Tadao Inogai (1908-1978) Kodokan 8th dan has, along with co-author Roland Habersetzer, several judo books, published in the French language, to his name.

57 Roland Habersetzer (born 1942) is a senior French practitioner of Japanese and Chinese martial arts and is the author of several reference books on multiple styles.

58 Similarly, Kime-no-kata still remains of great value, as it too teaches several core principles that remain directly relevant to judo and self-defense.
59 Any lack of appreciation of the powerful ideas in Kodokan Goshin-jutsu is often due to shortcomings in teaching.
60 The Budokwai [Society of the Martial Way], or to use its full official name The Budokwai (The Way of Knighthood Society), was founded in London in 1918 by Gunji Koizumi (1885-1965) Kodokan 8th dan, and initially offered tuition in *jujutsu* (later transitioning to judo) and *kendo* [way of the sword]. It is one of the oldest such societies (or clubs) in Europe. The name Budokwai, as opposed to Budokai, arises from the conversion of Japanese to the Roman alphabet using an earlier system of transliteration that the one commonly used today. To this day, the continued use of Budokwai remains the club's preference.
61 Kotani retired from the Kodokan in 1988 and returned to his home prefecture of Hyogo, in the Kansai region of Japan.
62 Takata himself could throw in any (360°) direction with hane-goshi.
63 Gendai budo are modern Japanese martial ways which were established after the Meiji Restoration of 1868.
64 RFEJYDA = Real Federación Española de Judo y Deportes Asociados = Royal Spanish Federation of Judo and Associated Sports—the NGB for judo in Spain.
65 The World Masters Judo Association (WMJA) was an entity founded in Ottawa, Canada in 1998 with the purpose of encouraging participation in competition judo and kata for "masters" judoka—that is, those aged 30 years plus, in a fun, friendly and family orientated manner. It "voluntarily disbanded" in 2010, ceding organisational control of masters' judo events to the IJF.
66 JBN = Judo Bond Nederland = Dutch Judo Federation—the NGB for judo in the Netherlands.
67 Two of the authors (LCJ and MPS) have personal experience, as uke, of the effectiveness of Cornish's Kodokan Goshin-jutsu, and are fully appreciative of the power of his technique.
68 The IJF have produced "competition formula" (IJF, 2015) that detail how many points to deduct for various categories of "mistakes" in a competitive kata performance. Consequently, when practising, judoka place great emphasis on avoiding these mistakes over and above any other aspects.
69 *Shu* is focused on the mechanical movements of a kata, and copying what a teacher shows. *Ha* involves developing a deeper understanding, by reflecting on the kata's principles after the mechanics have been learnt. *Ri* involves going beyond the original teachings, and developing personal variations based on the principles.

70 Ukichi (n.d.) cited in Daigo's (2008) lecture notes from the 2008 Kodokan Summer Kata Course, emphasises the *shu-ha-ri* approach to kata study.
71 Dax-Romswinkel (2015: 44) comments on a similar trend for Ju-no-kata, where its aesthetic component has faded due to the influence of kata competition.
72 USA Judo is the NGB for judo in the US.
73 The performance aspects of Kodokan Goshin-jutsu encompass its mechanical movements—including the timing and distance of individual techniques.
74 Note that the defense against the first staff attack—*furiage* [upswing against staff] is also launched before uke's strike. In this way the defenses against the attacks with the knife and the staff have some similarities.
75 A trained, suspicious and experienced gunman will not get within arms' reach of any opponent.
76 Combatives is a term for hand-to-hand combat training and techniques.

References

Blonk, M., DeBijl, R. and Van Dijk, F. (2010). *Kodokan Goshin Jutsu*. Den Haag: Paagman. (In Dutch).

Cornish, J.P. (1984). *Go-Shin-jutsu—Judo self defence kata*. United Kingdom: FJR Publishing for the British Judo Association.

Cornish, J.P. (1985). Koshiki-no-Kata. *British Judo Magazine*, 8(4), 6.

Cornish, J.P. (2004). What is Kata? *Kano Society—The Bulletin*, 10, 1-2.

Dabauza, P.R. (1988). *Kata Judo-Jujitsu*. Barcelona: Editorial Alas. (In Spanish).

Daigo, T. (2005). *Kodokan Judo—Throwing techniques*. Trans. F. White. Tokyo: Kodansha International.

Daigo, T. (2008). *Jigoro Kano—Kodokan Judo-no-Kata—Kodokan Published Showa 39* (1964). Lecture notes from the Kodokan Summer Kata Course, 29 July 2008. Tokyo: Kodokan Judo Institute.

Daigo, T. (2008-2009). Kodokan Judo Kata ni Tsuite (1)-(7) [About the Kata of Kodokan Judo—Parts 1-7]. *Judo*. 79(10), 52-57; 79(11), 7-12; 79(12), 18-23; 80(1), 16-22; 80(2), 43-50; 80(3), 12-16 and 80(4), 3-9. (In Japanese).

Dax-Romswinkel, W. (2015). Ju No Kata: The application of riai and its physical benefits. *Judoka Quarterly*, 1, 42-48

De Crée, C. and Jones, L. (2009). Kodokan Judo's Elusive Tenth Kata: The Go-no-kata—"Forms of Proper Use of Force" Parts 1-3, *Archives of Budo*, 5, 55-73; 75-82 and 83-95.

De Crée, C. and Jones L.C. (2011). Kodokan Judo's Inauspicious Ninth Kata: The Joshi goshiho—"Self-Defense Methods for Women" Parts 1-3.

Archives of Budo, 7(3), 105-123; 125-137; 139-158.

De Crée, C. (2016). Kodokan Judo's Three Orphaned Forms of Counter Techniques—Part 1: The Gonosen-no-kata—Forms of Post-Attack Initiative Counter Throws; Part 2: The Nage-waza ura-no-kata—Forms of Reversing Throwing Techniques; Part 3: The Katame-waza ura-no-kata—Forms of Reversing Controlling Techniques. *Archives of Budo, 11,* 93-123; 125-154; 155-171.

Draeger, D.F. (1973). *Classical bujutsu: The martial arts and ways of Japan volume 1.* New York: Weatherhill.

FFJDA. (n.d.) *Kodokan Goshinjutsu. Collection guide de judoka* (3). Talence: 4Trainer. (In French).

Finn, M. (1991). *Martial arts: A complete illustrated history.* Leicester: Blitz Editions.

Fraguas, J.M. (2001). *Karate masters.* California: Unique Publications.

Gatling, W.L. (2008). The First Kodokan Judo Kata International Competition and its katas. *Journal of Asian Martial Arts, 17*(1), 68-77.

Hamot, C., Pelletier, G. and Urvoy, C. (1985). *Katame no Kata Kodokan Goshin Jutsu.* Boulogne-Billancourt: SEDIREP. (In French).

Hoare, S.R. (2009). *A history of judo.* London: Yamagi Books.

Hoare, S.R. (2010). Go No Kata (The kata of resistance). Available online from URL: http://www.sydhoare.com/GO%20NO%20KATA.pdf

IJF (International Judo Federation—Kata Commission.) (2015). Kata Competition—Criteria for the Evaluation. International Judo Federation.

Inogai, T., author, and Habersetzer, R., compiler. (2007). *Judo kata—Les formes classiques du Kodokan.* Paris: Amphora. (In French).

Jomantas, N. (2009). Team USA to Compete at First Ever Kata World Championships This Weekend (13 October 2009). Available online from URL: http://judo.teamusa.org/news/article/28266 (Accessed: July 2010.)

Jones, L.C. and Hanon, M.J. (2010). The way of kata in Kodokan Judo. *Journal of Asian Martial Arts, 19*(4), 8-37.

Kano, J. (1934). The significance of judo and its objectives. In Imperial JapanOratory Society editors.

Budo Hokan [Martial Arts Treasures]. Tokyo: Imperial Japan Oratory Society Discussion Group. 290–294.

In Japanese

Kano, J. (1986). *Kodokan Judo.* Tokyo: Kodansha International.

Kano Sensei Biograpic Editorial Committee. (2009). Bennett, A. editor and translator. *Jigoro Kano and the Kodokan—An Innovative Response To Modernisation.* Tokyo: Kano Risei, Kodokan Judo Institute. English publication Tokyo: Bunkasha International Corporation.

Kano Society. (2006). Cornish, J.P. teacher. *Go-Shin-Jutsu—Part 1: Toshu* (against an unarmed attack); *Part 2: Buki* (against an armed attack). 2-part DVD set. London: Dial Media.

Kawamura, T. and Daigo, T. editors. (2000). *Kodokan new Japanese-English dictionary of Judo*. Tokyo: Kodokan Institute.

Kawaishi, M. (1956). Gailhat, J., editor. *Les katas complets de judo*. Paris: Impr. de J. Cario. (In French).

Kawaishi, M. (1957). Harrison, E.J., translator. *The complete 7 katas of judo*. London: W. Foulsham and Co. Ltd.

Kodokan. (1961). *Judo*. Osaka: Nunoi Shobo Co. Ltd.

Kodokan. (1976). *Illustrated Kodokan Judo*. Tokyo: Kodansha.

Kodokan. (1987 and 1992). *Kodokan Goshin-jutsu*. Tokyo: Kodokan. (In Japanese and English).

Kodokan. (1998). *Kodokan Judo kata series: Kodokan Goshin-jutsu*. VHS Edition. Tokyo: Kodokan,

Kodokan. (2004). *Kodokan Goshin-jutsu*. Tokyo: Kodokan. (In Japanese). https://www.hint.jp/cgi-bin/kshop/kshop.pl/page=bo021.html/SID =1440791991.47807

Kodokan. (2009). *Kodokan Judo kata series: Kodokan Goshin-jutsu*. DVD Edition. Tokyo: Kodokan, https://www.hint.jp/cgi-bin/kshop/kshop.pl/page=dvk06.html/SID=1440891385.48090http://kodokanjudoinstitute.org/en/waza/forms/textbook/

Kodokan. (2015). *Kodokan Goshin-jutsu*. Tokyo: Kodokan. Available online from URL: http://kodokanjudoinstitute.org/en/docs/goshin_jutsu.pdf (Accessed: March 2015)

Kotani, S., Osawa, Y. and Hirose, Y. (1968). *Kata of Kodokan Judo / Kata of Kodokan Judo revised*. Kobe: Koyano Bussan Kaisha Ltd.

Kotani, S. and Otaki, T. (1971). *Saishin judo no kata zen* [*The latest judo kata—Complete*]. Tokyo: Fumaido Shuppan. (In Japanese).

Kotani, S. and Otaki, T. authors. (1971). In Daigo, T. editor. (2008). *Kodokan Goshinjutsu* [from Saishin Judo no Kata Zen]. Reprinted for the 2008 Kodokan Kata Kaki Koshukai (Kodokan Summer Kata Course). Tokyo: Kodokan Judo Institute.

Kudo, K. (1967). *Dynamic judo: Throwing techniques*. Tokyo: Japan Publications Trading Company.

Kudo, K. (1967a). *Dynamic judo: Grappling techniques*. Tokyo: Japan Publications Trading Company.

Lindsay, T. and Kano, J. (1889). *Jiujutsu: The old samurai art of fighting without weapons*. Transactions of the Asiatic Society of Japan, XVI(II). Yokohama. 1915 reprint. 202-217.

Mifune, K. (1955). Mifune soen goshin-jutsu [Mifune's personal self-defense].

On: (2005). *Shingi Mifune Judan (Kanzenhan): Judo no Shinzui* [The divine Mifune 10th dan (complete edition): The Essence of Judo]. [DVD] Nihon Eiga Shinsha. Tokyo: Quest Co., Ltd. DVD SPD-3514, ca.: 06'21" (In Japanese).

Ochiai, T. (2012). Jones, L.C. and Mouri, O. translators. *Go-no-Kata*. Tokyo: Fuji Tosha-Do/Fuji Printing.

Oltremri, A. (n.d.). Takata Katsuyoshi 9°Dan: Hane Goshi. freeBudo. Available online from URL: http://www.freebudo.com/articoli/judo%20tradizionale/tecnica%20judo/23.takata%20hane%20goshi/Takata%20hane%20gohi.htm (Accessed: March 2008). (In Italian).

Otaki, T. and Draeger, D.F. (1983). *Judo formal techniques*. Tokyo: Charles E. Tuttle Company Incorporated.

Parulski, G.R. (1985). *Black belt judo*. Chicago: Contemporary Books, Inc.

Savage, M.P. (2010). *A brief history and appraisal of Kodokan Goshin Jutsu*. British Judo Association 2010 Technical Congress, Leicester.

Savage, M.P. (2013). Kodokan Goshin-Jutsu. *Judoka—Official Online Magazine of the British Judo Council*, 121. Available online from URL: http://www.judoka.britishjudocouncil.org/issue/18/april-2013-issue-121/335/kodokan-goshin-jutsu.html (Accessed: April 2015).

Savage, M.P. (2016). Jones, L.C. editor. *A brief history and appraisal of Kodokan Goshinjutsu* [Kodokan self-defence]. *Kano Society—The Bulletin*. Issue 28, 1-4.

Sharp, H. (2013). *Classic judo kata*. Los Angeles: Rising Sun Productions.

Shishida, F. (2010). Judo's techniques performed from a distance: The origin of Jigoro Kano's concept and its actualization by Kenji Tomiki, *Archives of Budo*, 6(4), 165-171.

Shishida, F. (2011). Jigoro Kano's pursuit of ideal judo and its succession: Judo's techniques performed from a distance. Ido Movement for Culture. *Journal of Martial Arts Anthropology*, 11(1-4), 42-48.

Shishida, F. (2012). A judo that incorporates kendo: Jigoro Kano's ideas and their theoretical development. *Archives of Budo*, 8(4), 225-233.

Shishida, F. (2013). How does the philosophy of martial arts manifest itself? Insights from Japanese martial arts. Ido Movement for Culture. *Journal of Martial Arts Anthropology*, 13(3), 29–36.

Stevens, J. (2013). *The way of judo—A portrait of Jigoro Kano and his students*. Boston: Shambhala Publications Inc.

Taira, S. (2009). *La essencia del judo: Volume 2—Kata, apéndices*. Satori Ediciones: Gijón. (In Spanish).

Takahashi, M. (and Family). (1995). *Mastering judo*. Tokyo: Champaign: Human Kinetics.

Takata, K. (1961). *Estudio del hanehoshi*. Argentina: La Imprenta López. (In

Spanish and English).

Tomiki, K. (1953). Goshin to shite judo ni tsuite [Concerning judo as self-defense]. *Judo*. May 1953. 45-49. (In Japanese).

Tomiki, K. (1956). *Judo, appendix: Aikido*. Tokyo: Japan Travel Bureau.

Tomiki, K. (1958). *Kodokan Goshin-jutsu*. Tokyo: Kodokan / Baseball Magazine. (In Japanese).

Ukichi, S. author (n.d.) Matsumoto, T. and Davidson, P. translators (n.d.) in Daigo, T. editor. (2008), *Eternal kendo*. Reprinted for the 2008 Kodokan Kata Kaki Koshukai (Kodokan Summer Kata Course). Tokyo: Kodokan Judo Institute.

Watanabe, K. (2003). *Essential judo katas*. Richmond Hill, Ontario: World Master Judo Association.

Watson, B.N. (2008). *Judo memoirs of Jigoro Kano*. Victoria: Trafford Publishing.

Yiannakis, L.M. with Cunningham, S.R. (2002). The kata of judo—Part I of a series. *American Judo—A Journal of the United States Judo Association*, Fall 2002: 19-21.

Yiannakis, L. with Cunningham, S.R. (2003). The kata of judo—Part II of a series. *American Judo—A Journal of the United States Judo Association*, Fall 2003: 20-24.

chapter 9

The Logic of Kodokan Judo Kata

by Llyr C. Jones, Ph.D.

This chapter is on Kodokan judo's *nage-no-kata* ("forms of throwing") and *katame-no-kata* ("forms of control"). Together, these katas form the *randori-no-kata* ("forms of free practice"), and their study helps facilitate the development of free practice (*randori*) skills.

During my formative years in judo, the emphasis in the United Kingdom was only on sports competitive judo, and kata practice had essentially been eliminated. There were no teachers with kata experience local to me, and so my early study of kata was self-directed through books. After developing competence in the mechanical movements of the randori-no-kata, I sought instruction from those judoka who had kept the kata flame alive in the UK, and over the years refined my skills under the guidance of some of the country's foremost kata experts, including Dai (David) Ball, the late Graham Wright, and Bob (Robert) Thomas. I would like to record my gratitude to those teachers now.

As an experienced judo player, I was privileged to develop further insight into katas through a memorable period of judo study in Japan. During my time spent at the Kodokan International Judo Institute in Tokyo and at various dojos in Kanagawa prefecture, I came to understand how the learning extractable from katas transcends that of merely developing physical skills and perfecting technique. While in Japan I cemented my belief that the link connecting judo's past, present, and future lies in the accurate teaching and practice of kata and it is this philosophy shapes my own kata practice, research, and teaching to this day.

Kata study is a challenging activity and achieving any degree of mastery will require many hours of patient and diligent study under the guidance of a knowledgeable teacher. However, as tips for their physical practice, the following elements should be considered essential. (In the following explanations, *tori* is the person who applies the technique, and *uke* is the person who receives the technique.)

- **Understanding**: An understanding of the fundamentals of the kata being demonstrated.
- **Logic**: Every movement in the kata must have a sensible purpose and be done in a sensible way. As such, one should always keep in mind the fundamental principles being demonstrated and the reason for the application of any particular technique.

- **Active Thought:** Katas should not be robotic, so one should actively think about one's role (as either tori or uke) and whether one is initiating or responding, attacking or defending, escaping or adjusting, etc.
- **Composure:** Proper concentration, decorum, and attitude.
- **Commitment:** Real attacks and real defenses.
- **Tempo:** Each kata has its own speed and tempo. Within some (e.g., the nage-no-kata) the tempo also varies from move to move, while others have one tempo.
- **Fluidity:** The kata must "flow" since any performance will break down if there is hesitation during application.
- **Posture:** Balance and body control.
- **Coordination:** Between tori and uke in the techniques themselves, but also in the movements and transition between techniques.
- **Positioning:** Awareness of one's location on the mat with proper engagement distance, direction, and spacing.
- ***Reigei:*** Correct etiquette.

Kata practice should go beyond merely performing physical movements, and during practice one should always think about how kata can improve one's judo in the broader sense. The following are tips on assimilating and leveraging the lessons of randori-no-kata into everyday judo.

▶ **Nage-no-Kata:** Consisting of five sets of three throws, each performed to the left and right sides, this kata helps develop an understanding of the theoretical basis of judo and the processes involved in *kuzushi*, *tsukuri*, and *kake*—i.e., how to assume the correct position for applying a throwing technique once uke's balance has been broken, and how to apply and complete a technique. This kata has uke attacking tori fifteen times—each time learning and adjusting his attack based on tori's previous response. Tori neutralizes uke's attack each time by applying himself and using the force or action of the attack itself to prevail. Tori also learns how his own body and mind react under physical and psychological stress, and also how to adapt effectively to changing circumstances utilizing both his body and mind.

▶ **Katame-no-Kata:** Consisting of three sets of five grappling techniques, this kata helps develop an understanding of the theoretical basis for learning control through executing and evading each technique. Tori learns how to best use his body in an efficient manner to control uke on the ground through working on his versatility and body movement while grappling. Similarly, uke, through striving to escape, learns how to exploit any weaknesses in tori's technique. Each and every time the katame-no-kata is practiced, uke should continue to test tori by looking for his weak points and then attacking them, while tori should find new ways of nullifying uke's new escape attempts.

Sequence 1

1a) Shoulder wheel (*kata-guruma*) from the first set—hand techniques (*te waza*). 1b) Lift-pull hip throw (*tsurikomi-goshi*) from the second set—hip techniques (*koshi waza*). 1c) Inner-thigh throw (*uchi mata*) from the third set—leg techniques (*ashi waza*). 1d) Rear throw (*ura nage*) from the fourth set—supine sacrifice techniques (*ma sutemi waza*). 1e) Side hook (*yoko-gake*) from the fifth set— side sacrifice techniques (*yoko sutemi waza*).

Sequence 1
is from a nage-no-kata
performance at the
First Kodokan Judo Kata
International Tournament, 2007.

Tori: Katsuyuki Kondo, sixth dan.
Uke: Tetsushi Okouchi, fifth dan.

Sequence 2

2a) Broken top four-corner hold (*kuzure kami shiho-gatame*) from the first set—holding techniques (*osaekomi-waza*). **2b)** Naked lock (*hadaka-jime*) from the second set—strangling techniques (*shime-waza*). **2c)** Arm crush (*ude gatame*) from the third set—joint techniques (*kansetsu waza*).

Sequence 2
is from a katame-no-kata
performance at the
First Kodokan Judo Kata
International Tournament, 2007.

Tori: Kazutaka Yamamoto, seventh dan.
Uke: Hirao Nasu, sixth dan.

*All photographs copyright Carl De Crée
(2007) and used with permission.*

index

advanced foot sweep (de ashi barai), 91
aiki-jujutsu, 106, 114, 140
aikido, 106, 111, 113, 128, 131, 137
All-Japan Judo Federation, 35-36, 58, 112, 147
almost ippon (wazari), 27-28
Araki-ryu, 112
Araki, Muninsai, 112
archery techniques (kyu-jutsu), 112
arm crush (*ude gatame*), 161
arm crushing armpit armlock (ude-hishigi-waki-gatame), 124, 130
arm crushing hand armlock (ude-hishigi-te-gatame), 139, 150
arm crushing stomach armlock (ude-hishigi-hara-gatame), 108
armed attacks (buki-no-bu), 120, 122, 126, 131-132, 134-135
armlock (kote hineri), 14
arresting art (taiho-jutsu), 140
attacked from a distance (Hanareta-baai), 120-121, 126, 135
Awazu, Shozo, 5
back-carry throw (seoi-nage), 49, 84, 91
balance breaking (kuzushi), 48, 73, 76, 84, 92, 96, 113, 125, 129-130, 132, 146, 150
basic technique (kihon), 37
being gentle and pure (seiboku), 56, 65
Blonk, Mas, 144
body control (tai-sabaki), 5, 12, 48, 86, 107, 125, 127, 129-130, 132, 149-150
break-falling (ukemi), 24, 95
British Judo Association (BJA), 8-9, 20, 57
broken top four-corner hold (*kuzure kami shiho-gatame*), 161
Budokwai (London), 45, 137, 141
choking techniques (shime-waza), 6 note 3, 124, 161
circle throw (tomoe-nage), 2-3, 5, 59-60
commitment (genshitsu), 56, 65
comprehensive martial arts (sogo bujutsu), 112
contest (shiai), 1, 6, 10, 19, 27-29, 37, 45, 58, 107
continuousness (renzoku), 74-76, 89, 92
controlling techniques (katame waza), 107, 124-125, 129, 132, 143
Cornish, John, 65 note 4, 102, 118-119, 121, 124-125, 130, 136-138, 145-146

counterattacking techniques (kaeshi-waza), 5
Cuevas, Jorge, 141
Dabauza, Pedro Rodríguez, 141
Daigo, Toshiro, 5, 6 note 5, 40, 42, 46, 56, 59-60, 65 note 5, 102-103, 105, 140
de Bijl, Richard, 144
distance control (maai), 74, 125-126, 129
double foot sweep (okuri ashi barai), 92
downward cut (kirioroshi), 32
downward slash (kirikomi), 108
downswing (furi-oroshi), 120, 122
eight directions unbalancing (happo-no-kuzushi), 125
etiquette (reiho), 119, 133, 161
European Judo Union (EJU), 42, 57
floating drop (uki-otoshi), 49
following or countering (gonosen), 96, 117
forms of decision (Kime Shiki), 46, 52, 103, 118
free practice (randori), 5, 10, 18-19, 25-26, 36-37, 41, 44, 89, 101, 103, 106-107, 117, 126, 129, 160-161
Fujoshi Goshin Jutsu no Kata, 117-118
Fukuda, Hashinosuke, 23
generating momentum (hazumi), 73-74
Giunta, Jeff, 40-41
Go-no-kata, 12, 46-47, 50-51, 102, 105, 117-118, 123
Gokyu-no-waza, 26, 71, 78, 80-81, 84, 103-104
Goshin-jutsu, 12-14, 47, 50, 100, 104, 106, 114, 117-118, 137-138, 144
Goshin Waza, 96, 104, 106, 117
Goto, Ichizo, 1-3, 5
grade advancement (batsugun), 28
grappling techniques (ne-waza), 3, 23
grasping hands (torite), 110
Greater Japan Martial Virtue Society, 107
Habersetzer, Roland, 128, 143
halberd techniques (naginata-jutsu), 112
Hamana, Tomoo, 147
hand techniques (*te waza*)
Hirohito, Michinomiya (Emperor), 41
Hoare, Syd, 45, 105
holding techniques (osaewaza), 6 note 3, 161
horse-riding techniques (ba-jutsu), 112
Iikubo, Tsunetoshi, 23
Iizuka, Kunizaburo, 2-5

168

immovable mind (fudoshin), 52, 65
initiative strategies (sen), 74
inner thigh throw (uchi-mata), 5, 96, 160
International Judo Federation (IJF), 8, 29, 31, 45, 57-58, 66 notes 13 and 15, 147-149
International Olympic Committee (IOC), 30
International Sports Federation, 31
Isogai, Hajime, 2, 4-5
Itsutsu-no-kata, 47-48, 52-53, 66 note 10, 102, 123, 141
jigotai, 87
Job, Michael, 40
joint-locking technique (kansetsu-waza), 6 note 3, 124, 161
Jomantas, Nicole, 60-61, 148
Joshi Goshin Ho, 46-47, 50, 65, 110, 116, 118
Ju-no-kata (flexible form), 12-13, 35, 37, 40-41, 98
Ju Shiki, 46, 52, 103
jujutsu, 8, 10, 20, 23-25, 33, 36-37, 41-42, 44, 51-52, 96, 100, 107, 110, 112, 114, 141
Kaeshi-no-kata, 12
kake, 63, 73, 92
Kano, Jigoro, 4, 8, 20, 22-23, 35-36, 43-44, 47-48, 52, 56, 58, 62-63, 65 note 6, 100, 103, 105, 128, 139
Kano, Risei, 5, 114
Kano Society, 145
Kano, Yukimitsu, 36, 66 note 16
Katame-no-kata (grappling form), 11-12, 18, 37, 39, 47, 49-50, 98, 102, 105-106, 123, 138, 143, 149, 160-161
Kawabe, Kazuhiko, 139
Kawaishi, Mikonosuke, 5, 116
Kime-no-kata (decision form), 12, 32, 37-38, 52, 108, 116-117, 138
Kito Kata, 53
Kito-ryu Jujutsu, 12, 23, 25, 37, 44, 53, 56, 65, 110
knee strike (hiza-ate), 129
kneeling (idori), 107-108
Kodokan All-Japan Kata Competition, 41
Koshiki-no-kata, 12-13, 47-48, 52-53, 63-64, 66 note 10, 102, 104-105, 123, 141
Kotani, Sumiyuki, 2-3, 100, 102, 109-111, 118-119, 122, 124, 136-137, 140, 146-147
Koyasu, Masao, 109, 134
Kudo, Kazuzo, 109-110
Kuhara, Yoshiyuki, 118
Kumitsukareta-baai, 121
Kurihara, Tamio, 1-3, 5, 100, 109-110

large outer reap (osoto-gari), 5, 90, 92, 96
large wheel throw (oguruma), 80, 84, 91
leading (sen sen no sen), 96
lectures (kogi), 44, 101
leg techniques (ashi waza), 160
leg wheel (ashi guruma), 4, 80, 84
Leggett, Trevor, 13, 45, 98, 137
lift-pull hip throw (tsurikomi-goshi), 160
lifting (tsuri), 79
lifting-drawing foot sweep (harai tsurikomi ashi), 92
major hip throw (ogoshi), 84, 91
major outer drop twist (osoto-otoshi), 121
major outer wheel throw (osoto-guruma), 81, 84
Masamoto, Iso, 23
maximum efficiency (seiryoku zen'yo), 24, 84, 103, 115
Mifune, Kyuzo, 1-2, 4, 56, 66 note 12, 100, 106, 109-110, 114
minor outer hooking throw (ko soto gake), 92-93
Mochizuki, Minoru, 106
modern martial ways (shin budo), 25
Murata, Naoki, 41-42, 45, 63
Musashi, Miyamoto, 85, 99
Nagaoka, Hideichi, 100, 108-110
Nagaoka, Shuichi, 2, 4-5
Nage-no-kata (throwing forms), 12, 47, 49, 59-60, 77, 84, 102-105, 123, 149, 160-161
Nakano, Shozo, 100, 109-110
naked choke (hadaka-jime), 124, 160
no-mindness (mushin), 54-55, 125
Nogaki, Paul, 56
Oba, Hideo, 128, 134
Ochiai, Toshiyasu, 118
Oltremari, Alessio, 45, 57-58
Olympic judo, 8, 13, 22, 30-32, 42
Omori, Chigusa, 40
Onozawa, Koshi, 40, 141-142, 145
opportunity (debana), 48, 65
optimization (sei-ryoku), 56
Osawa, Yoshimi, 136
Oshu-no-bu, 134
Otaki, Tadao, 100, 109-110, 137
Pan-Am Judo Union, 41
partnered practice (sotai renshu), 51
Parulski, George, 138
Pelletier, Guy, 54-55, 138
pistol at the back (haimen-zuke), 120, 122, 127-129, 133, 135, 139
pistol attacks (kenju-no-baai), 120, 122
practice drills (uchi-komi), 10, 26, 94-95, 130

Randori-no-kata, 18, 47, 49, 53, 119
rear sacrifice techniques (ma-sutemi-waza), 59
rear throw (*ura nage*), 160
remaining mind (zanshin), 48, 65, 125
renraku waza, 92
Rentai-no-kata (forms of physical education), 50, 53
repetitive throwing practice (nagekomi), 94
rhythm (hyoshi), 85
Ri-no-kata (forms of theory), 52-53, 56
Rommelmann, Heiko, 40-41
Roosevelt, Theodore, 4
Russo, Miguel, 40
Samura, Kaichiro, 2-3, 5, 100, 110, 114
Sato, Masaru, 119, 122
Sei'ichi Shirai, 110
Sei-ryoku-zen'yo Kokumin-Taiiku, 46-47, 102-103
Sengoku, Tsueno, 122, 139-140
sense of positioning (tsukuri), 48, 63, 65, 71, 73, 86, 92
Shinken Shobu-no-kata (combat forms), 12, 32
Shinmeisho-no-waza (newly accepted techniques), 104
Shobu-no-kata (kata of self-defense), 12, 50, 53
short staff techniques (jo-jutsu), 109, 112, 114
shoulder wheel (kata-guruma), 49, 160
shu-ha-ri (educational process), 55, 148
side hook (*yoko-gake*), 160
side sacrifice throw (yoko-sutemi), 2-5, 160
side separation throw (yoko wakare), 91
side thrust (yoko-tsuki), 108
side wheel throw (yoko guruma), 84, 91
single-wing choke (kataha-jime), 108
slanting strike (naname-uchi), 120-121
solo practice (tandoku renshu), 51
Sone, Taizo, 91
Sosuishi-ryu, 106, 112
Sosuishitsu-ryu, 106, 112
spear techniques (so-jutsu), 112
staff techniques (bo-jutsu), 112, 114, 120, 122, 131-133, 138, 152
standing techniques (tachiai), 108, 123-124
striking techniques (atemi waza), 12, 23, 96
Sugiyama, Shoji, 40
supine sacrifice techniques (*ma sutemi waza*), 160
Suzuki, Kiyoji, 134
Suzuki, Kiyoshi, 109
sweeping loin throw (harai goshi), 91
swimming techniques (sui-jutsu), 112
sword techniques (ken-jutsu), 112

sword unsheathing (nuki-gake), 108
Tabata Shotaro, 1-2, 5
Taira, Shu, 143-144
Takahashi, Toshimitsu, 41
Takeda, Jiro, 106
Takenaka-ha, 53
Takenouchi, Hisamori, 112
Takeuchi Santo-ryu, 110, 112
Tanto-no-baai (knife attacks), 120, 122, 149
Tenshin Shin'yo-ryu, 23, 25, 37, 39
throwing techniques (nage waza), 23, 26, 129
Tokyo Metropolitan Police Department, 41, 140, 151
Tomiki, Kenji, 100, 106, 109-115, 123, 125-128, 132-134, 137-138, 145-146, 148, 150-151, 153
traditional 18 martial arts (bugei juhappan), 112
traditional school (koryu), 100, 107, 110, 112, 140
Tsue-no-baai (staff attacks), 120, 122, 132, 135
two-hands hold (ryote dori), 14
Ueshiba, Morihei, 106, 112, 114
unarmed attacks (toshi-no-bu), 120-121, 139
underlying principles (riai), 103, 130, 132
undivided attention (senshin), 56, 65
uppercut (ago tsuki), 14
van Dijk, Ferry, 144
Waseda University, 112, 114, 127, 133, 153
water wheel (mizu guruma), 14
Waza no Ri, 63
World Masters Judo Association (WMJA), 57, 141
wrist reversal (kote-gaeshi), 127-128, 147
wrist techniques (tekubi-waza), 110
Yagyu, Munenori, 89
Yagyu Shinkage-ryu, 89
Yamashita Yoshitsugu, 2-4, 108-109
Yamazaki, Masayoshi, 147
Yoda, Fumikazu, 41
Yokoyama, Estuko, 40
Yokoyama, Sakujiro, 3
Yoshimatsu, Yoshihiko, 5, 6 note 4
Yoshin-ryu, 44, 65

Printed in Great Britain
by Amazon